Date Due			

7 VOCATIONAL PERSPECTIVES SERIES

1

alba house ■ DIVISION OF THE SOCIETY OF ST. PAUL
STATEN ISLAND, N.Y. 10314

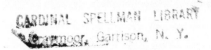

ECCLESIAL WOMEN

Towards a Theology of the Religious State

Thomas Dubay, S.M.

NIHIL OBSTAT:
  Daniel V. Flynn, J.C.D.
  Censor Librorum

IMPRIMATUR:
  Joseph P. O'Brien, S.T.D.
  Vicar General, New York
  October 30, 1969

The nihil obstat and imprimatur are official declarations that a book or pamphlet is free of doctrinal or moral error. No implication is contained therein that those who have granted the nihil obstat and imprimatur agree with the contents, opinions or statements expressed.

Library of Congress Catalog Card Number: 77-110589

SBN: 8189-0162-4

Designed, printed and bound in the U.S.A. by the Pauline Fathers and Brothers of the Society of St. Paul at Staten Island, New York as a part of their communications apostolate.

PREFACE

Life runs deeply. Religious life runs deeply. The problems of religious life run deeply, much more so than many of us think. The positions we take regarding poverty, community, habit, hierarchical direction, celibate love are profoundly influenced by our presuppositions as to what exactly we are as religious. It is regrettable that these presuppositions often remain tacit. Were we aware of our unexpressed assumptions and unspoken premises we might expect the real issues to emerge more clearly than they do. Real issues tend to spark realistic thinking.

In the daily press and in community bulletins, in television interviews and in small group conversations, in retreat discussions and periodical articles we see and hear religious pronouncing on their communal problems with little apparent awareness of the real roots of their remarks. Yet to address oneself to these difficulties without a sound theological knowledge of this particular life style is like approaching the practical problems of nursing without understanding the basic principles of human health. Do not some of our more vocal observers deal with religious congregations as though these were chiefly if not solely sociological-psychological phenomena? Governmental and poverty matters are viewed quite aside from an ecclesial context, much as a giant business corporation would view them. The concepts of prayer and work together with their inner relationships are discussed without apparent reference to the ecclesiality of contemplation and the hierarchical direction of apostolate. Nor do we always find a seriously worked out and non-selective biblical basis for these discussions. Yet a religious is evangelical or she is not. Further, we submit that she is ecclesial or she is not. Though she may personally be a saint, yet if she is not evangelical-ecclesial, she is not the woman of whom the four documents of Vatican II speak so beautifully.

Our purpose here is far from merely academic. Dialoging and chapter decisions must be based on sound theology or we will renew ourselves out of existence. And considerable contemporary evidence shows that this is no idle threat. We had better know who we are and what we are about among the people of God. Any being succeeds according as it is faithful to its own inner evolving nature. Ducks flourish only as ducks. Religious flourish only as religious.

A contribution to successful renewal, however, is not our only purpose in these pages. The unique person looms large. The consecrated virgin, we say, is a woman of love, universal, warm love. If this is so, she is distinguished in the people of God first and foremost by interpersonal relations to the Lord and to His people. We diminish her personal dignity if we describe her primarily by her function. Machines are solely functionary. Persons may have noble functions to fulfill, but they are never first of all dentists or librarians or engineers. They are before all else drinkers of beauty, lovers of God and other persons. To say that the virgin stands in deep and intimate interpersonal relationships to the Lord and to His people is to say that she is by nature ecclesial. We understand her full beauty only when we understand that she is an ecclesial woman.

Russell College
Burlingame, California

CONTENTS

Chapter Two

FUNCTIONAL ECCLESIALITY OF THE RELIGIOUS
WOMAN / 35

ABBREVIATIONS

CC	Dogmatic Constitution on the Church
CDR	Dogmatic Constitution on Divine Revelation
CL	Constitution on the Sacred Liturgy
CCMW	Pastoral Constitution on the Church in the Modern World
DMSC	Decree on the Media of Social Communications
DE	Decree on Ecumenism
DERC	Decree on the Eastern Rite Churches
DPOB	Decree on the Pastoral Office of Bishops in the Church
DPT	Decree on Priestly Training
DRL	Decree on the Appropriate Renewal of Religious Life
DLA	Decree on the Lay Apostolate
DMLP	Decree on the Ministry and Life of Priests
DMAC	Decree on the Missionary Activity of the Church
DCE	Declaration on Christian Education
DRCN	Declaration on the Relation of the Church to Non-Christian Religions
DRF	Declaration on Religious Freedom

ECCLESIAL WOMEN:
THEOLOGICAL ROOTS

It has become commonplace for theologians and journalists to remark that Vatican Council II was a beginning, not an ending, an invitation to development of doctrine, not a final formulation of it. Of the many areas in contemporary theology in which this observation is true that of the religious life is not the least conspicuous illustration. So conspicuous is this example, in fact, that there has been more than a little grumbling about the sparsity of new ideas in the conciliar thinking about the gospel life of the counsels. Yet invitations are there, many of them. It is up to us to bring the buds to bloom.

Conciliar Beckoning

Of these invitations perhaps the one most frequently offered is that we consider religious as ecclesial persons. This suggestion occurs in several documents and from numerous points of view. Religious are given birth and grow in the field of the Church (CC #43; DMAC #18; DRL #1). Their profession is a *special* consecration which is deeply rooted in their baptismal consecration and more fully manifests it (DRL #5). This profession commits them to the service of God in a *new* way and *more intimately* for it is a "more inward consecration" to Him (CC #44; DMAC #18). Religious women (and men) live the life of the Church in a *particular* way (CC #43) and they belong to the diocesan family in a *special* manner (DPOB #34).[1] Sisters are joined to the Church in a *special* way through the evangelical counsels and enjoy a *firmer* commitment to her ministry (CC #44; DRL #14). They do not belong to the hierarchical structure but do *belong inseparably* to her life and holiness (CC #44), and foster that holiness in a *special* manner (CC #42). Contemplative religious life belongs to the *fullness* of the Church's presence and its members are her glory (DMAC #18; DRL #7). In their good works religious congregations make the Church experienced for those works are not privately done — they are discharged *in her name* (DRL # 1, 8). Sisters *identify* with the Church in *all* her undertakings and live her very life. So true is this that their living and thinking with her is always to be on the increase (DRL #2, 6).

Religious women are likewise ecclesial witnesses in the thinking of Vatican II — not just witnesses in general, but witnesses in, for and of the *Church*. They are a testimony for the Church to mankind at large (CC #46; DMAC #18; DRL #1), and yet serve in the same capacity to the other members within Christ's Body (CC #44, 46), for they manifest and signify in a *luminous manner* the very nature of the Christian vocation (DMAC #18). We are told that religious adorn the Bride of Christ (the Church) and make her radiantly beautiful for her Spouse (CC #46; DRL #1). They are a *"better symbol"* of the union between Christ and His Church (CC #44; DRL #12). The way of the evangelical counsels shows wondrously the boundless power of the Holy Spirit working in the Church (CC #44).

Sisters appear as women of the Church, finally, in their officially mandated apostolates. Repeatedly the council speaks of them as furthering the mission, welfare, expansion of the Church by their *total* dedication to her (CC #43, 44, 46; DPOB #33; DMAC #15, 18; DRL #1, 5, 6, 10, 14, 20). Religious congregations have played and still do play a very large role in the evangelization of mankind (DMAC #40); they have borne the burden and the heat of the day in their missionary labors in the *name of the Church* (DMAC #27). They hand on to pagan nations the treasures of mysticism they possess (DMAC #18). Even the canonical fact of exemption (greater or lesser) is aimed at the good of the Universal Church. We are reminded that the reason congregations can be removed from the jurisdiction of local bishops and subjected to the pope alone is the benefit they can thus afford to the entire flock of the Lord (CC #45; DPOB #35). It could hardly be said more plainly: religious are ecclesial.

Meaning of Ecclesiality

When we say a sister is an ecclesial woman, what exactly are we saying? Is the expression merely pious? Or does it suggest simply that she works in and for the *"Ecclesia"?* Or could it reflect some deeper reality, something ontological, something imbedded in her very being as a consecrated woman? Answers to these questions may well begin with the word "ecclesial." What does ecclesial mean?

This adjective is, of course, directly derived from the Latin, *ecclesia* (church), and the Greek, *ekklesia* (legislative or deliberative assembly of a city, especially Athens). "This assembly included only the citizens who enjoyed full rights, and thus the word implies both the dignity of the members and the legality of the assembly." [2] This Greek word was used to translate the Hebrew *qahal,* the solemn assembly of God's people, and in the New Testament it was applied both to the local community and to the universal group of those who believed in Christ. To say, therefore, that a religious woman is ecclesial is to say she is related to the Church. In this sense, of course, every woman (and man) related to Christ is related to the Church, and so we are suggesting more, namely, that the sister is related to the *qahal Yahweh* in new and deeper ways . . . precisely insofar as she is a religious.

It becomes apparent, then, that the more profoundly one

understands what the Church is, the more profoundly will he understand what and who a religious is. Yet it is not easy to say what the Church is. No one definition can enclose her. No one image depicts her. She is mysterious, profoundly mysterious, but in such a way that we can know something of her, even though that something will never become everything.

The Church is a people, a people called together by God, a people to whom he addresses his word and in that word purifies them into his own bosom. This people is a spiritual dwelling in whom He abides in a wonderful, hidden, new way, a way not shared with the rest of creation. These people are living stones and become themselves collectively, the single temple on earth in which Father, Son and Spirit dwell. They are the body of Christ into whom He sends His Spirit Who animates this body as its soul, its supreme principle of life and unity. They are a pilgrim people making their way in poverty under the sign of the cross.

This people is a communion, a love-gathered group, made up of those who believe together, aspire after the same goods together, worship together, love together. They live by two principles, charismatic and hierarchical, and it is the Spirit alone who guarantees that the two will work in ultimate harmony. The *ekklesia* of Christ is essentially made up of a series of dualisms, incarnational-eschatological dualisms. She is human and divine, visible and invisible, eager to act and devoted to contemplation, present in this world but not at home in it.[3] Her human members do not exhaust her nature, because she is vivified by a divine Spirit. We do not try to explain her, therefore, simply by describing and criticizing her human members, lofty or lowly. She is tangible, visible, sacramental, but eye has not seen nor ear heard the invisible realities she encloses in her bosom. She acts in an intricately complex and varied apostolate but, at the same time, she is dedicated to the solitary contemplation of her Lord. She is present on this earth but as a stranger, a pilgrim, for she aspires after her home in heaven.

If the Church is all this (a people, dwelling, temple, body, spirited-communion, pilgrim, charismatic, hierarchical, human-divine, visible-invisible, active-contemplative, earthly-heavenly), she is a mystery or she is nothing. And still we have not pointed out all her unfathomable traits: virginity, motherhood, spouse, field, sheepfold, vineyard. No one image describes her adequately; human words cannot encapsulate her whole being. Yet we are calling the sister an ecclesial woman, a woman of the Church, and it is to all of this that we are referring. Even though these pages do not deal professedly with the Church, we trust that our two core concepts, religious woman and Church, will mutually illuminate each other as we proceed.

Religious as Ecclesial

We may ask what precisely we are suggesting when we assert that the consecrated woman is ecclesial. Does this expression merely indicate a functional dedication, a full-time concern with the Church's tasks in the world? Does it mean that the sister's way of life finds its concrete origin in the hierarchical approval that makes it to be and that this manner of living is regulated by this same structure? Or does the virgin's ecclesiality refer also to some reality imbedded in her being? The ecclesiality of the evangelically vowed woman means all of these: a hierarchically authenticated way of life, a theological reality in her very own person, a functional commitment to an apostolate. We have organized our reflections on this basis.

Chapter One - ontological ecclesiality: religious women share more deeply in the very nature of the Church (e.g., as the people of the transcendent — immanent God, as temple, communion, sacrament, virgin-bride, mother, pilgrim).

Transcendental Woman

Man is either defined in terms of God
or he is not defined. Other visible realities can be adequately
categorized, essentialized, defined, because they are only matter
and matter can be placed in intellectual boxes. Insofar as man
is a bodily being he, too, can be boxed in by a definition, a
distinguishing and setting-limits-to. We put him (rightly, for
otherwise science could not exist) into all sorts of intellectually
dissected boxes: matter, extension, parts — atoms, molecules,
tissues, — tall, stout, beautiful, — instinct, emotion, imagination — German, Polynesian, pigmy — male, female. But insofar as man is spirit he cannot be encapsulated. He is an
insatiable pursuer of infinity. This biped alone in the vast cosmos is dissatisfied with any and every particular experience,
and yet he never gives up seeking new and other experiences.
If he is an intellectual, he invariably wants to read another book,
hear this other lecture, attend that next convention. If he is
a playboy, his life is one mad series of parties, trips, affairs.
Food must always be better, jokes funnier, clothes richer, sex
sexier.

Man is voracious. And he is voracious not because he is
animal but because he is spirit. Mere animals are quite content
with the same lodging, unexotic food, humdrum mating. They
have no spirit. They are boxed in by finite matter. But this
curious human phenomenon is incarnated spirit incapable of
encapsulation. He is constantly bursting beyond himself, beyond

the sphere of the particular, beyond the reach of the limited. Buried deep within him is a secret dynamism that drives him beyond every object into the bosom of the Silent who is no object, who surpasses every object and all of them together. Only man in the vast cosmos is unsatisfied with the cosmos and thirsts for its origin. Only he could think of shouting: "I stretch out my hands, like thirsty ground I yearn for you." [4] His secret dynamism is the key to the human puzzle. It is his spirit.

How do we know that man is a pursuer of infinity? We see his being pointed to the limitless not only on the level of sense experiences. We see it also in his drive toward understanding. Man supposes that everything makes sense, or at least that it should make sense. This is to say that he assumes everything has a reason behind it, or should have a reason. Man is an incurable metaphysician. Even the materialist who tries to show why there is no such thing as metaphysics supposes that "why" makes sense, that there are reasons for his position. He is a metaphysician in the very act of denying metaphysics. All of us possess this inner drive toward intelligibility and we cannot shake it loose. When the physicist attempts to explain the electron shells of an atom, he supposes an intelligibility, an order, a design in it. He supposes the shells make sense. And once a person assumes intelligibility, order, design, he has assumed an intellect, an orderer, a designer. (What book writes itself?) Even more. In every affirmation a man makes (e.g., "lightning causes thunder, rivers flow, this toothpaste is mint-flavored"), he affirms a supreme origin for his unqualified assumptions (principle of contradiction — mint is not non-mint — sufficient reason, order, beauty). If these assumptions are correct, it is only on condition that there be a fontal Reason, Orderer, Beauty, Intelligible rather than a supreme absurdity, ugliness, tricker. In every affirmation man points out of himself into the Absolute, into the endless Mystery that is God. He supposes intelligibility and he pursues it . . . without limit.

The same basic pursuit is present in man's insatiable quest

for happiness. Men differ in their judgments as to what produces happiness, but they are utterly alike in their conviction that it must be pursued. It is this drive for happiness that literally makes men go. It is the hidden spring that sends a woman shopping for a new dress, a man to the race track. It is the inner energy that explains why a heart patient consents to an operation, why a student studies, a salesman sells, a monk prays. It is that interior yearning that knows no enough. And this never knowing enough is itself a gaping openness whose only adequate explanation is the divine Adequacy.

For these reasons (and others unmentioned) we say that man is *by nature* transcendent. As spirit he cannot be enclosed either in himself or in this finite world. He is either defined in terms of God or he is not defined.

So far we have been speaking of man as he exists by nature. But this is not the whole story. It is only a presupposition of the whole story, for there is no such thing as a concrete, here-and-now merely natural man. A man of pure nature is a mere abstraction. Real, existential men, *this* man and *that* one, have been touched by the saving grace of Christ. They live in an undeserved, supernatural economy and are destined to the triune God of the beatific vision. Actual men are naturally transcendent, yes, but their inborn bursting out toward the Absolute has itself been grace-orientated. It is not merely directed to an unlimited horizon but into the very bosom of Father, Son and Spirit. Of his gracious loving goodness the Lord has decided to be himself, in his own inner life, the answer to the gaping question that man is.

To understand the sister as a transcendent woman, therefore, we need to grasp not only what man is but also something more about the beyondness of this God toward whom man is as a matter of fact orientated by his human nature. What does the transcendence of God imply? It implies that he is unspeakably beyond the created order. And we mean "unspeakably" in the literal, sober sense, not as a pious exaggeration.

God is not simply one being next to others. He is not merely
the greatest, the loveliest of all. He is the source and the purpose of them all, unendingly surpassing any one of them and
all of them together. He is all this and yet so transcendent that
he is also "merciful, tenderhearted, slow to anger, very loving,
and universally kind; Yahweh's tenderness embraces all his
creatures . . . (He) acts only out of love." In the same hymn
we hear of this tender God, "Can anyone measure the magnificence of Yahweh the great, and his inexpressible grandeur?" [5]
    The divine transcendence means that God does not *possess*
perfections as we do. He does not simply have more power,
goodness, knowledge, joy, love than any other. He *is* pure
power, subsistent beauty, complete self-awareness, sheerest delight, utter love itself. He is justice and mercy, power and
goodness, knowledge and love and joy without any confusion,
contradiction, diminution. He is incomprehensibly beyond created goodnesses.
    So true is all of this that any idea we have of this God is
more unlike him than like him. Our idea may be correct and
represent some glimmer of this God, but it forever remains a
poverty-stricken glimmer. The most exalted intellectual vision
of a Teresa of Avila is a mere babbling about the divine reality,
a babbling that leaves unsaid immeasurably more than it says.
The divine transcendence means precisely that: whatever we
can know or say of our God necessarily fails to contain the
whole reality. Only the uncreated Word images the Father
completely. This is why Augustine could say that if you understand, it is not God.
    Divine transcendence, therefore, is an absolute mystery that
forever outstrips our latest formulations. We have here one
reason that theology can forever grow and develop. The ancient Hebrew knew of this radical, inexhaustible transcendence
"Can *anyone* measure the magnificence of Yahweh the great,
and his *inexpressible grandeur?*" [6] St. Paul spoke of it when
he proclaimed that the King of kings and Lord of lords, the

only Sovereign dwells in "light inaccessible." [7] Any man must know of it, speak of it, live it or he is not dealing with the real God. True enough it is that this transcendent Mystery is also immanent, more within us than we are within ourselves. True it is that he has chosen to speak himself visibly, tangibly in his Word made flesh. True enough it is that we have seen his glory in his enfleshed Word,[8] that we have looked upon and handled the Word of life that has appeared to us.[9] True it is that we as incarnated spirits cannot go to God as though we were disembodied angels. Yet for all this it remains that the Father is radical mystery, completely other, purest subsistent All. To humanize this God, to make him like unto us (rather than us unto him), to regard him as a buddy-buddy pal does not appeal to modern man. It does not appeal because it is phoney. A buddy-buddy God is no God.

Now here is where the sister comes in. She is incarnated, enfleshed. She is in the world, among and of the people of God. She is a flesh and blood pilgrim among fellow pilgrims. She is a very picture of the pilgrim Church, "present in this world but not at home in it." [10] In her whole being and way of life she points to the unspeakable Beyond. Her virginal consecration makes no sense except in terms of this Beyond.

Once we see man as an insatiable pursuer of infinity, an incarnated spirit who defies definition, a striking being who, unlike any other, is unsatisfied with any particular experience and all of them taken together, we then begin to see the virgin as a beautiful symbol of what being human really means.[11]

If it is true that man always and necessarily bursts beyond himself, then she is a glory to humankind who points so plainly to this Beyond. The layman in his temporal, secular vocation tells of the goodness of creation. He reminds all the people of God of their tasks in this world and of their incarnated status. He is the symbol of man as pinnacle of the cosmos. The religious woman tells all the people of God that buried deeply within each of them is a secret dynamism, their spirit, that drives them to the radical Origin of the cosmos, the Sacred. The sister's eternal, sacred vocation is directly pointed to the bosom of the Silent: Father, Son, Spirit. She is a beacon within God's people enlightening first by what she is and only secondly by what she does. Being precedes doing. The virgin is an ecclesially transcendent woman. She proclaims to the people of God that the center of their existence has been shifted out of this world into the holy bosom of the triune God.

Sacred Woman

If the religious is a transcendent woman, she is a sacred woman. She is reserved for the sphere of the Holy One. Even if she is a member of a congregation devoted to an external apostolate, she still remains sacred. A sister is not a secular person any more than Paul, immersed to his ears in apostolic activity, was a secular person. Both Scripture (e.g., Lk 18:29-30) and the magisterium support the common theological concept of the essence of religious life as including the idea of a withdrawal from the world. What this withdrawal implies we shall later indicate. That the religious lives in and for the sphere of the sacred is repeatedly insisted upon in the documents of Vatican Council II. She seeks the good of the Church "*primarily* by means of prayer, works of penance, and the example of (her) own life." [12] Every woman, of course, points beyond herself or she would be sub-human. She is dynamically orientated to the unlimited, beyond the particular this and that. The married woman, however, *as married,* is concerned with things, particular things of the tangible, calculable world, how she may please her husband. The virgin, on the other hand, as a consecrated person is concerned primarily with the unlimited, the intangible, the deep other side of reality, how she may please the Lord. True, she deals with things in the specified here-and-now of this world, she has her feet firmly fixed on the planet earth, but her whole raison d'etre *as virgin* is the absolute mystery of God: how she may be plunged ever more deeply into it herself and how she may aid others in being

so plunged. A sister who views herself first as a teacher or nurse
or social worker has her theology backwards. She does not know
who she is. She is "to live for God alone not only by dying to
sin but also by renouncing the world . . ." and for this reason
she must "combine contemplation with apostolic love." [13] She
is a woman of the sacred sphere. And that is the sphere of the
Church.

Woman of Divine Immanence

Because of our unavoidable human
proclivity to think with spatial imagery, one can only too easily
conclude from an exposition of Yahweh's transcendence that
his limitless beyondness renders him remote from the tangible
world of men and things. To say that he is unspeakably beyond
the created order suggests that he is not within the created
order. To assert that he is not simply one more being (even
the greatest) next to other beings but the very ground of them all
may seem to imply impersonality. To explain that no human
formulation can ever exhaust him, that *any* created idea is
more unlike than like him seems to remove him from the human
sphere altogether. If no one can measure "the magnificence of
Yahweh the great, his *inexpressible* grandeur," how can anyone speak of him correctly? How can we know we are dealing
with a real God? Is he relevant to us?

Furthermore, we have said that the whole being of the
consecrated virgin is pointed to the unspeakable beyond, the
things of the Lord. We have insisted that her sacred vocation
is plainly orientated to the bosom of the holy, silent One, the
One who can never be encapsulated in human words, enclosed
in the limited and particular. We have said that she is a transcendent and therefore a sacred woman. Are we now going to
affirm that she is a woman of immanence in the world, she
who has somehow left the world?

Yes, this is what we are affirming. But we must begin not
with her but with God. On the surface of the matter it may

seem impossible that Yahweh be both beyond and within, both higher than the clouds and in the deepest recesses of the earth, both transcendent and immanent. Part of our problem derives from our human situation: we are enfleshed beings and we can think only as enfleshed beings. Even our sublimest immaterial thought is accompanied by material imagery. "Beyond" and "within" are for us first of all spatial ideas. But when we speak of God, "beyond" does not mean first of all spatial distance, nor does "within" primarily bespeak an enclosed center. We are using quantitative terms to explain unquantitative realities, the relations of created things to their uncreated source. The divine immanence, God's withinness, refers, on the natural level, to his omnipresence to all things, a presence that pours out their entire being and their activities from their deepest centers. It is the presence of Yahweh forming in secret the psalmist's body in the womb of his mother, the presence of him in whom we live and move and have our being.[14] On the supernatural level this withinness is the divine indwelling of the new revelation. The abiding presence of Father, Son and Spirit in the graced man is a new immanence. It is not merely a creative presence but an intersubjective communion with a created beloved. The new man and his God know, love, enjoy and possess each other in an interindwelling. If a man will only love, the Father will send his Spirit into him to dwell forever, and the Father with his Son will come to abide in that man and manifest themselves to him.[15] God abides in man and man abides in God.[16] This new immanence is the focal point of man's destiny: he is made to commune intimately with the Love ("God *is* love") lodged in his deepest center. This thrust is found repeatedly in the pages of the Old Testament. Man is to be sensitive to the awesome presence of the Lord: "Yahweh is in his holy temple; let the whole earth be silent before him." [17] He meditates on the Lord day and night; he seeks him like parched earth; he thirsts for him like the weary doe.[18] The incarnate Son "*always* goes off to some place where he can be alone and pray" [19] to his Father who dwells within him,[20] and he tells his followers to pray at all times.[21] This obscure continual converse through faith here below is destined to cede to clear uninterrupted vision hereafter, for admittedly we see now darkly as in a mirror but then face to face. Now we know partially, but then totally.[22] And that is eternal living: to know (for the Hebrew "to know someone" is to experience him deeply — a man "knows" his wife in sexual intercourse) the one true God and Jesus, his Son.[23] This culmination of human-divine indwelling intersubjectivity surpasses our wildest imaginings, for it is what God has prepared for those who love him.[24]

We have said that the sister is a woman of divine immanence in the world. She who points in her every being to the beyond-God also points to the within-God. How can this be? By her triple evangelical consecration she clearly reaffirms her baptismal relocating of her being outside this world in the very bosom of the triune God. She is clearly a symbol of divine transcendence of mundane existence. How can we now affirm that this same triune dedication orientates her to the divine immanence? Once we divest transcendence and immanence of their spatial suggestions our problem is solved. Not only is there no clash between Yahweh higher than the clouds and in the deepest earth, but the one perfection utterly demands the other. If our God is unspeakably within all reality, it is only because he unspeakably surpasses it. So also the religious woman, but perhaps we should assert the relation in reverse order. Because she points in her person to the bosom of Father, Son and Spirit utterly beyond the confines of this (or any) creation, she points to her very own bosom, for this God has chosen to lodge there in a peculiar interpersonal intimacy with her. This beyond God is found within. Because the consecrated woman is a symbol of the one she is also a symbol of the other.

Ecclesial Temple

The Church as edifice is adorned in Sacred Scripture by various names: "house of God (1 Tim 3:

15) in which dwells his family, the household of God in the Spirit (Eph 2:19-22); the dwelling place of God among men (Apoc 21:3); and, especially, the holy temple." [25] St. Paul speaks of the Corinthians (in the plural) as the one temple of God.[26] Of all places of the vast cosmos in which the Lord God wishes to dwell the place par excellence is within his own people, within his Church. The stones of the ancient temple were dead, while those of the new are living.[27]

Among the living stones the one best suited to symbolize the whole Temple-Church is the virgin.[28] She bears a virginal-feminine relationship to Christ just as the Church does, and both are dedicated to him alone. The presence of the Spirit of Christ in his Temple-Church obviously is not a static, impersonal relationship. It is above all an intersubjective, mutual presence and as such implies knowing, loving, enjoying. The Lord is an acting Lord and the people in whom he acts are to be a responding people. If one reads carefully the scriptural account of this response, he notices that the absorbing and absolute character of it is best seen in the virgin whose sole concern is the Lord alone.[29] All men are to find their basic rest in Yahweh alone.[30] The virgin has chosen no other. All are to pursue him with all their heart.[31] This is her obvious aim. Every man is to seek the Lord so vehemently that he can speak of thirsting, pining, longing, yearning for his God.[32] The virgin is a virgin in order to do precisely this with an undivided heart. All men have as their ideal to converse with the Lord continually, day and night.[33] The virgin is what she is that she may pray without distraction.[34] If it is true that "it is of the *essence* of the Church that she be both . . . eager to act and devoted to contemplation," [35] no one can evade the conclusion that she whose vocation is to be totally concerned with the things of the Lord in service and in contemplation is the ideal symbol of this Church.

All this offers adequate basis for understanding the astonishing hierarchy of ecclesial functions that Vatican II assigns to religious. Most people speak as though the first task of religious

in the world is to work on behalf of men. It is not. Not only
is it true for any man that "action is subordinated to contemplation," [36] but it is also true that what the Church wants first
of all from religious are prayer, penance, example of sanctity.
An external apostolate comes second. "It is their duty to
foster these objectives (of upbuilding the Mystical Body)
primarily by means of prayer, works of penance, and the example of their own life.... They should *also* enter more
vigorously into the external works of the apostolate." [37] Even
working religious are assumed to be "thoroughly enriched with
the treasures of mysticism," [38] and the mystical treasure par
excellence is advanced contemplation, a divinely-originated and
profound communion with one's indwelling Lord. By her vocation, therefore, the religious woman is ideally suited to symbolize the Church in whom the Spirit dwells as in his chosen
Temple. She of all men most easily proclaims to her inabiding
Lord: "I look to no one else in heaven. I delight in nothing else
on earth. My flesh and my heart are pining with love, my
heart's Rock, my own, God forever... My joy lies in being
close to God." [39]

Church as Communion

Recent work in ecclesiology has been
at pains to de-emphasize structural elements in the Church
in favor of insisting upon the communitarian aspects of her
life. This work has both prepared for and followed from the
ecclesiology of Vatican II, which ecclesiology repeatedly refers
to God's people in terms of interpersonal relations: fellowship,
community, society, communion, Messianic people, holy nation, priestly community, God's family, assembly of love, a
unity of faith, hope, love, an admirable brotherhood, a marvel-
ous communion. If the Church is so plainly a family communion of living and loving together, if religious life luminously
manifests the inner nature of the Christian vocation (DMAC
#18), and if the religious community is a "true family gathered

together in the Lord's name" (DRL #15), one can easily see why the religious congregation should be a miniature *ecclesia,* an assembly of love on a small scale that is a picture of the assembly of love on a large scale.

The New Testament presents an astonishing picture of the Church as communion in love. We read that early Christians greeted one another with "kisses of love." [40] They longed to see one another and when they did meet, their mutual presence brought joy.[41] Their love was apparently so deep it occasionally brought tears.[42] The apostles' correspondence was replete with terms of endearment, terms that would make some of us feel ill at ease were we to use them: God's beloved, brothers, beloved to me, dearest children, dearest son, you are in our hearts, very dear children, my beloved, beloved and longed for, my joy, most dear to us, our glory and joy, beloved son, my dear children, little ones.[43] It is true enough that, following the example of Jesus in his occasional stern correction as well as in his usual affectionate manner, the apostles were capable of firm decisions and hard words. Yet the admonitions on how Christians are to correct the erring (apparently the non-malicious erring) are both singularly free of harshness and characterized by advice to show a warm, forgiving love. After counseling the Corinthians not to be too severe in correcting a culprit, Paul has only three positive bits of advice on how to deal with him: forgive, comfort, show love to him.[44] The Apostle advises the Galatians "to *instruct*" gently the man caught doing something wrong, supposing in the wrong-doer good faith plus a simple unawareness of what he is doing.[45] The same counsel of gentleness is directed to Timothy when the latter deals with those who resist him.[46] All this is simply living the forgiveness of the loving father who corrected his son with an embrace, a kiss and not a single word of reproach.[47] Whatever else we may call this manner of dealing with human sin and blunder we are going to have to call it warm and affectionate.

This is part of what we mean when we say that the New Testament presents an astonishing report of the early Church

as a communion in love.[48] Early Christians — at least many
of them — did take literally their charge to incarnate God's
love, to make it appear in tangible, visible form. After all, they
(and we) had been told that their love was to be so extraordinary that it was to be a sort of miraculous proof that the
incarnation had taken place: this kind of communion could
be explained only on the supposition that God himself had
appeared in human flesh.[49] The Church is this communion.
It is an assembly of love before it is anything else.

Religious Communion

How does the religious woman fit into
this image of the Church? Is a convent an ecclesial communion
in some significant way, some manner over and above that of
any other group of Christians? We have already recalled that
the religious life luminously manifests the inner nature of the
Christian calling (DMAC #18) and that a religious community is a "family gathered together in the Lord's name"
(DRL #15). The religious woman is a member of *an* ecclesial
communion within and manifestive of *the* ecclesial communion
which is the Church. She is freely bound together with a group
of evangelically orientated persons who propose to believe
together, hope together, worship together, live together, love
together in an intensively total Christian manner. Yet this miniature communion is not isolated from the universal communion
any more than families are isolated because they are distinct
from one another. It is a communion with its own specific
differences, of course, and to look for unity of religious with
the whole people of God by supposing identity of the lay and
religious vocations is like seeking man's individual unity by
denying any significant difference between an eye and a finger.
How well the religious community mirrors the universal ecclesial community is perhaps best seen in the primitive descrip-
tion of the infant church found in Acts 2:42-47:

These remained faithful
    to the teaching of the apostles,
    to the brotherhood,
    to the breaking of bread
    and to the prayers . . . .
The faithful
    all lived together
    and owned everything in common . . . .
They went as a body to the Temple every
day
        but met in their houses
        for the breaking of bread.
They shared their food gladly and gene-
rously;
    They praised God
        and were looked up to by everyone.

The religious communion is a communion of contemplation
and apostolic love, of voluntary factual poverty and committed
loving celibacy; of Spirit-originated freedom joined to Spirit-
prompted obedience to authority, of presence in this world but
pilgrimage toward another. Because they are members of this
miniature *ecclesia,* sisters must be at pains to grow into warm,
loving women. Communion bespeaks intersubjective closeness.
Although it would be unreal to expect every religious to be
deeply related to many others, it is crucial that they share with
all to at least a reasonable extent, and that they show an ob-
servable warmth to every companion.

Shown universal love is primary in any Christian community,
but if the community is to have an effective form of apostolic
orientation, the secondary element of authority must also be
present. And it is here that we find a characteristic trait of
religious community as distinguished from other groups within
the people of God. Authority in religious life is unlike that
in the natural family or the state. For these latter the governing
power originates in a natural relationship and/or the consent

of the governed and in this sense ultimately derives from God. In the religious institute, on the other hand, governing competence (a pastoral power, not a "lording it over" the brethren) derives from the Church, since the institute exists as religious only because of the Church. Religious are mandated by the Church, are totally committed to her apostolate, and therefore enjoy a share in her jurisdiction.[50] A religious congregation is consequently an ecclesial communion in a sense not shared by the natural family or the layman's organization.

The ecclesiality of this communion shines out in yet other ways: organized liturgical prayer, Spirit-originated charisms of dedicated virginity, voluntary poverty, works of mercy (such as teaching, counseling, healing), contemplation, etc. What the sister does she does as a member of a team, an ecclesial team. Even when she researches alone in a library, keeps lonely vigil at a bedside, communes with her God in solitary prayer she is still a community-woman and therefore an ecclesial woman.

Sacrament of Salvation

The whole present divine economy is sacramental. Yahweh has sacramentalized his thoughts in words, his will in deeds, his fullness of being in countless beings. Everything shouts the divine. The very Sacrament of God, Christ Jesus, has sacramentalized his people — he has made them both sign and vehicle of his saving graciousness on earth. He has enfleshed his redemptive power in a Church that is both a sign and a cause of salvation. She is a sign-cause of new life in a world that has grown old and weary and jaded. Whether this pilgrim people is moving slowly into a condition of diaspora is not clear. Yet there is evidence that deeply committed Christians faithfully clinging to Peter are becoming fewer and fewer in a world population that is growing larger and larger. If the Church of the future is to be made up of scattered pockets of the faithful, her sacramentality may stand out even more prominently. Signs generally are not coextensive in space to the realities signified. The Church of the diaspora (and to some extent we are already in a diaspora situation in many areas) does not probably touch large segments of a population, and yet it can influence the teeming populations by its simple bodily presence in their midst. It stands out to men as God's grace in tangible, historical presence. And the more this sacrament of salvation is renewed, holy, and Spirit-driven, the more it stands out, the more it is a sign, a sacrament.

It is at this point that the religious woman appears prominently in our sacramental picture. She does not bestow the seven intense actualizations of the Church's grace giving essence, but she does stand before the world as both cause and effect of the vivifying Spirit who makes men to live the filial life of Christ Jesus. A sister proclaims the Church's holiness in her flesh, a holiness not only in word and sacrament as means of grace, but an achieved holiness due to God's power, a power which is not only promised to be victorious but which actually is now victorious in her. She is a tangible witness to the fruits of the Spirit-Soul of the Mystical Body: love, joy, peace, kindness, goodness, faith, continence, modesty.[51] She presents to the whole world an increasingly clearer revelation of Christ . . .

> contemplating on the mountain,
> announcing God's kingdom to the multitude,
> healing the sick and the maimed,
> turning sinners to wholesome fruit,
> blessing children,
> doing good to all,
> and always obeying the will of the Father who sent Him.[52]

This sacramental function of the religious woman is rendered
all the more effective through a habit that combines an attractive modernity with an unmistakable mark of consecration.
Her way of life is tailor-made to manifest the multi-faceted
life of Christ: his contemplative solitudes, his teaching, healing,
doing good to all, his virginity, poverty, obedience to the Father.
If he is salvation in the flesh and the Church is .sacrament of
Christ, the religious woman of all women is best suited by her
vocation to represent this Church in her role as sacrament of
salvation. It goes without saying that the sister's effectiveness
as ecclesial sacrament is conditioned by the warmth of her love,
the depth of her prayer, the enthusiasm of her activity. For it
seems that the Church as sacrament is closely tied in with the
Church as communion. Is it not true that the world is to know
who the disciples are by their love for one another? [53]

Pilgrim Poor

The new people of God, like the old,
are "pilgrims and strangers on earth," [54] "present in this world
but not at home in it." [55] Taking these words at their face
value and in their stark reality is a scandal to contemporary
ears. One cannot easily evade the conclusion that they assert
much that seems incompatible with sundry strands in the rosy
movement toward secularism. To state that man is a stranger
on earth is a stark statement by any standard. Not only do
social customs, advertising, monetary outlays assume that man
is (or ought to be) very much at home on his planet, but theology itself as it loses its scriptural soul only too frequently tends
to the secularistic interpretation of man and cosmos.

Right it is that man is man in *this world*. Correct it is that
this incarnated spirit must work out his destiny on the stage
he has been given, not some other. True it is that man must
love this visible universe, improve it, bring it to completion.
Yet the stark biblical and ecclesial statements remain: man
is a stranger on earth, not at home. Before we attempt to re-

concile these assertions we may profitably notice that the second is not at all as forbidding as it first appears to be. In point of fact the contradictory assertion is icy. And Sartre and Camus have proven it. Their writings are eloquent witnesses to the fact that if man indeed is at home on earth, both he and it are absurd. If one looks at the tragedies of life through secular glasses and without distracting himself into believing they are only partially real, he cannot avoid despair. We may leave aside the obvious tragedies: starvation, drug corruption, tortures of war, destruction of beautiful innocence, lack of love. The bold fact of death is proof enough of our point. The gaping infinity that is man cannot tolerate the notion of a final destruction of his being. Even if this world were an unclouded, rosy utopia, and especially if it were such, death seems to man an intolerable destiny. If this world were all, all becomes nothing. It is only because our destiny lies beyond this concrete situation that this concrete situation takes on a strange new beauty. What was from a purely secular vantage point huge and hostile becomes in the light of Yahweh, the mysterious, warm and friendly. We pilgrims can be thankful that we "are present in this world, yet not at home in it." We can be thankful that our home is nothing less than the bosom of Father, Son, Spirit.

What does it mean to be a pilgrim Church? We may first ask what it means to be a simple pilgrim. Besides being one who has his goal elsewhere — a pilgrim is not a mere nomad (he has a goal) — a pilgrim is one on a quest. He is on the road. He is searching, seeking. His pursuit is not just any pursuit — it is a resolute pursuit of the sacred. A pilgrim is poor — he travels lightly. He sees beauties on the way but he does not rest in them.

What is the pilgrim Church? Perhaps we can best answer this question with biblical answers and at the same time understand why the religious woman is so apt an image for it.

The pilgrim Church is a questing people. We seek and we long, we pine and we thirst, and we are not satisfied. We know what we seek, but we do not see it. We know whom we want, but we rarely enjoy Him. Yet we pursue. "You are my God, I am seeking you, my soul is thirsting for you, my flesh is longing for you, a land parched, weary and waterless." [56] The raison d'etre of the sister's vocation is pursuit, free, ardent, untrammeled pursuit of her Beloved. She readily represents a people on the move, a people whose center is nowhere visible because it is the bosom of the Trinity, a people who seek but are unsatisfied.

The pilgrim Church is a restless people who have only one haven. The destiny being sought is not merely one among others. It is not even the best among others. It is the sole destiny, the only rest: "In God alone there is rest for my soul . . . I look to no one else in heaven, I delight in nothing else on earth." [57] Of all this people the consecrated woman most obviously looks to no one but her God; she most emphatically seeks rest and delight in no other. Most fully can she say "my joy lies in being close to God." [58]

The pilgrim Church is a poor Church, poor both in fact and in spirit. It is poor because pilgrims typically travel lightly; they cannot be impeded on the way. It is poor because its pilgrim Master had no place to lay his head and he charged the twelve to "take nothing for the journey: neither staff, nor haversack, nor bread, nor money; and let none of you take a spare tunic." [59] Paul was able to say he possessed nothing [60] and he admonished Timothy to avoid superfluities and be content with adequate food and clothing.[61] Vatican II speaks of the Church as poor herself,[62] as showing a preference for poor people.[63] The council admonishes bishops to have simple dwellings,[64] invites priests to embrace voluntary poverty and to give away what they do not need,[65] tells religious to be poor in fact as well as in spirit.[66] Even the laity as well as others are reminded to pursue detachment from material goods and to give to the poor not only of their superfluities but even of their necessities.[67] While everyone of the people of God are to appear as pilgrim signs as well as be such, the poor virgin is by profession best suited to reflect the poverty of her pilgrim people. Being concerned with the things of the Lord, she is not concerned with catching the eyes of men with her dress; her recreation is refreshing but unworldly; her food is simple, even poor. The virgin must obviously be an eschatological woman, a woman of faith whose whole concern is the pursuit of her Lord.

The pilgrim Church is a stranger on earth.[68] While it is present in this world, it is not at home in it.[69] This people has its goal and final rest elsewhere. It minds the things that are above, not the things of this earth.[70] It looks not to the passing trials of this age but to the weight of glory that is eternal.[71] To escape the reproach that this view of man on earth fosters an unconcern with human progress, some observers speak as though Scripture and Vatican II do not really say these things. It is more real and honest to assert plainly (as Christ did) that we are not of this world,[72] that we are strangers here.[73] Yet at the same time we are deeply involved in our pilgrimage, in improving the way, in loving and caring for our fellow travelers, in bringing this earth to its completion, even in preparing for a new earth. The religious woman is obviously all of this. Her very clothes indicates that she is destined for the beyond, that she is not of this world as Jesus was not of it. Yet all the while she is deeply involved in serving her fellow pilgrims, teaching them the saving truth, healing their illnesses, caring for the helpless and the aged, and especially loving with a universal love. Like the genuine pilgrim whose heart is elsewhere, she rejoices as though not rejoicing, buys as though not possessing, uses this world as though not using it. This world is passing away and she is free from care.[74] The virgin is the picture of a pilgrim. As such she is thoroughly ecclesial.

Virgin Church

We encounter at this point a semantic problem: how relevant and meaningful in today's world are the terms, virgin, bride, spouse, mother, when applied to the Church and (especially) to the religious woman? On the one hand there are reasons for discarding them as out of date in a technological and sophisticated society. The religious woman appears to many much more as a professional career woman than as a bride or mother. With today's heavy emphasis on the goodness and attractiveness of sex the idea of virginity strikes many as a half-life. And the other terms, bride, spouse, mother, when applied to the sister seem to be an unreal attempt to romanticize religious life, to promise a girl the very things she is giving up, and to promise them in a tenuous, unhuman manner.

On the other hand there are reasons of no little consequence supporting a continued use of all four words when speaking of the Church and the religious woman. The first reason is that this terminology is thoroughly biblical, concrete, existential. If we are living in an age of biblical renewal and existential personalism, one would expect that age to welcome a phraseology that avoided the speculative, abstract, essential. How completely scriptural these terms are may be seen from a few examples. We read of Yahweh, "Like a young man marrying a virgin, so will the one who built you wed you, and as the bridegroom rejoices in his bride, so will your God rejoice in you." [75] Says Paul of the Corinthians, "I arranged for you to marry Christ so that I might give you away as a chaste virgin to this one husband." [76] In Ephesians the apostle relates at length Christ to the Church as a husband is related to his wife.[77] And as we shall show below, New Testament writers teach a spiritual parenthood by which a man (and presumably a woman too) can beget real offspring.[78] We can hardly leave aside this kind of biblical legacy.

A second reason is the simple fact that "virgin, bride, mother" do express the glories of woman as woman. Unless one wants to view the religious woman as asexual, as unrelated intimately with any man, as a mere careerist, what is he going to call her? Is he going to strip her of what makes a woman beautiful: a refreshing purity, a wedded relationship, a fruit-ful motherhood?

The crucial reason for retaining these terms is basically that they express facts, and one cannot argue facts away. Most religious *are* virgins, and virginity is the fullest expression of a consecrated chastity. They *are* wedded to Christ (as we shall show below) — what else can we call this state? They *are* mothers in the order of redemption (again, as we shall show below), and we do not yet have a better word for mother. Now, one may of course ask, if all this is so, why do these terms seem out of date, unreal? We submit that the real problem here is not the terms, but the listeners or readers. Any terminology (e.g., in medicine, law, philosophy) is meaningless to one who does not understand its history and its import. Who could study the Yahweh-Israel marriage theme of the Old Testament and not be struck with its beauty and appropriateness for express-ing a profound knowing-loving-delighting intimacy between God and men? Who could study deeply the theology of con-secrated virginity and not want to call a sister a virgin? Who could study the theology of apostolate and prayer and man's part in the conferring of grace and not want to speak of father-hood and motherhood? Who could study the heights of divinely originated contemplation and not want to call that transform-ing union a marriage union? What is really needed here is more study and better preaching.

The scriptural roots giving life to the concept of the Church as the virgin-bride of Christ run deep. The marriage theme be-tween Yahweh and his people finds frequent expression in the old dispensation. His relations with his chosen ones are to be so intimate that he chooses wedded union as a symbol to express them. Israel is no longer to be forsaken but shall hear from the lips of the Lord the remarkable promise: "You shall be called 'My Delight' and your land 'The Wedded'; for Yahweh takes delight in you and your land will have its wedding. Like a young man marrying a virgin, so will the one who built you wed you, and as the bridegroom rejoices in his bride, so

will your God rejoice in you." [79] This marital love is absolute
and exclusive, it suffers no competition: "*One* thing I ask of
Yahweh, *one* thing I seek: to live in the house of Yahweh
all the days of my life, to enjoy the sweetness of Yahweh [80]...
In God *alone* there is rest for my soul." [81] The Lord knows
his bride in the vivid Hebrew sense of a mutual experience
in one's whole being: "How good Yahweh is — only taste and
see [82]... Rejoice, exult with all your heart... He will exult
with joy over you, he will renew you by his love." [83] This is
the language of bride and groom. It is also the language of the
Old Testament: God's people are his bride.

In the new dispensation the same theme continues, though
now the incarnated Son is the groom and the Church is his
bride. This Church is betrothed to one spouse; she is the chaste
virgin presented to Christ.[84] So genuine is this marital relationship that it is a model for husbands and wives in their mutual
love, respect and care.[85]

For long centuries Catholic thinking has seen a wedded
relationship of some sort between the consecrated virgin and
Christ. Most likely this tradition can trace its origin to St.
Paul who sets his treatment of Christian virginity in a marriage
context and even relates the virgin to Christ as the wife is related to her husband.[86] This same theme is found in early
patristic literature and in the fourth-century rite of the consecration of virgins, a rite that resembles our marriage ceremony.
Our present day liturgy continues and even emphasizes the
bridal character of the religious woman. The sainted virgin
is greeted at vespers as "spouse of Christ" and the new Mass
for the profession of religious women has the marriage theme
running throughout. One who denies the bridal character of
consecrated virginity is either uninformed or he is unimpressed
with the Church's obvious mind.

The fourth manner (our other three: Yahweh-his people,
Christ-Church, Christ-individual virgin) in which Christian
tradition sees a marital relationship between God and man is

the transforming union of contemplative prayer. We have already noted how Vatican II without the least apology placidly supposes that everyone knows that working religious are to be "thoroughly enriched with the treasures of mysticism." [87] A *thorough* enrichment can only mean a fullness, and a fullness of mystical contemplation (the mystical treasure par excellence) is what we call the spiritual marriage. This expression, spiritual marriage, signifies a profound interpersonal union between man and his indwelling God, the most profound union possible on earth. It is perhaps the type of union St. Paul had in mind when in a context dealing with the sexual union of man and woman he spoke of the person who clings to the Lord as being "one spirit with him."[88] If a modern theology of marriage is correct in emphasizing the intersubjective love relationship between husband and wife more strongly than bygone ages did, a theology of contemplation has been and is correct in its calling the deepest intersubjective God-and-man relationship a spiritual marriage.

Now it is interesting to observe that the consecrated virgin alone, of all persons in the Church, can claim to be a bride in all of our four senses. She is completely an ecclesial bride. As a member of the Church she shares in the Yahweh-Israel relationship and in its fulfillment, Christ and the Church. She alone is the virgin who is concerned wholly "with the things of the Lord." And the primary purpose of her virginal life is contemplative prayer-love and therefore its fullness, the spiritual marriage.[89] She is completely an ecclesial bride.

Even before examining the data of revelation and the mind of the magisterium we could have expected on a priori grounds that the sister should enjoy a bridal relationship with God, or, as Ambrose put it sixteen centuries ago, that a "virgin is a woman wedded to God." [90] If the Church is a virgin bride in the integrity of her faith, hope and love, and if the sister is so entirely an ecclesial woman, she too must be a virgin bride. Needless to say, we have here another reason why the religious woman must be utterly a woman of God, another basis for her difference from the laywoman. Of all the people of God the sister should say most unstintingly: "I look to no one else in heaven, I delight in nothing else on earth . . . My joy lies in being close to God." [91] Just as the good wife has eyes for no other than her husband, so the virgin has eyes for no one but Christ. While she loves everyone deeply and intensely and warmly, her exclusive love is centered on her Christ alone.

We have here, too, another reason why an external apostolate, good and even crucial as it is, is not the primary reason for the virginal consecration. The religious who is a religious chiefly if not solely to teach or nurse or work in a slum does not understand what being a religious really means. She does not grasp the thinking of Vatican II that a religious is in a diocese *primarily* (the very term the council uses) to pray, to do penance and to give an example of sanctity. [92] Startling as this observation may be at first sight, it is nothing more than a recognition that victorious grace operating in a man's heart is before all else an invisible working of the Lord within his deepest center and only secondarily the work of a human instrument. To support the contrary position (namely, that a religious is in the local Church primarily to work) is to suppose that salvation is first man's work and then God's. It is also to suppose that the religious must first love her neighbor and then herself, whereas Scripture has it that we love our neighbor *as ourselves.*

Mother Church

Like her most exalted member, the Church is not only a virgin; she is also mother. She unites the double feminine glory of perfect integrity and maternal fruitfulness. The new revelation speaks in terms of our being born again, a second time, [93] of our being created anew, [94] of our being renewed and regenerated by the Holy Spirit, [95] of our being reborn of incorruptible seed. [96] Through her preaching word, her sacramental works, her suffering members, her intercessory prayer this virgin Church is a supernatural mother of men. Like her head, she has come that men may have life and have it more abundantly.[97]

The consecrated woman has also come for the sake of life, not only that she may live and live fully in her intersubjective communion with her Beloved dwelling in her personal center, but also that she may communicate life to others. She is a virgin that men may live and live more abundantly. She is a virgin mother.

True it is that she does not bestow life through the hierarchical ministry of preaching and sacrament, but this by no means suggests that she does not bestow life. She mothers life in her own manner. She does not preach from the pulpit, but she does beget in her teaching and can say with St. Paul to her children, "It was I who begot you in Christ Jesus by preaching the Good News." [98] With St. John she can speak of her "dear children," her "little ones," her "beloved," because through her apostolate she has brought life to them.[99] Through her sacrifices and sufferings she has been in labor again forming Christ in her offspring.[100] Through her contemplative prayer she is energy in the bosom of the Church, a life-begetting energy that makes her to be a mother.[101]

The ontological rank of virginal motherhood derives from the ontological rank of the life it communicates. Just as the marital maternity on the natural level incomparably surpasses any sub-human fecundity because the human mother cooperates in bestowing intellectual, immortal life, so does a virginal maternity on the supernatural level unspeakably surpass the natural. As the liturgy of Holy Saturday night puts it, what benefit would it be to be born if we had not been redeemed? The motherhood of the virgin insofar as it is ecclesial (which is to say that it participates in the fecundity of the Church and is an expression of that fecundity) penetrates into the divine order, the order of the infinite, the order of an immediate and enthralling embrace with Father, Son and Spirit directly seen, loved, enjoyed. She is mother on the level of that reality which eye has not seen nor ear heard, a level so lofty that it has not entered into the heart of man to imagine it.[102] She begets in the order of the gloriously risen body, a body which in beauty and splendor far surpasses the bodies she would have begotten in an earthly marriage. The virgin's fruitfulness issues in off-spring whose bodies are *by her motherly activity* incorruptible, shining, agile, spiritualized, bodies patterned after the very risen body of Christ Jesus.[103] The virgin's motherhood, like the Church's, knows no bereavement, for her children know no death. It spans oceans and continents in a fruitfulness that defies numbering. Her motherhood enjoys tranquil purity, no disturbance of the flesh,[104] no division of the heart,[105] no distraction from prayer.[106] The religious woman is thoroughly a woman, a woman who, like Mary and the Church, rejoices in her two feminine glories, virginity and maternity.

Yet to whom much is given, much is required.[107] If a mother is a woman who bestows life on another, prolongs herself in another, is preoccupied with the other, she is by defini-tion altruistic. And if the virgin's children defy numeration and if her maternal influence spans the seas, she needs a heart wider and deeper than does the wife. She is a universal lover and needs a universal heart. The virgin has left all to love all. She should be the warmest of women.

If the religious woman glories in virginity and motherhood, we would expect a rich fulfillment in her. Any divinely originated vocation fulfills when it is generously lived, but this one does so in an especial manner. The religious has many more men and women to love and she is loved by many more in turn. Her chastity affords the fullest scope to her capacity for love. One may call it a vow of love. If her contemplation grows as it ought, she attains an abiding delight that literally surpasses understanding.[108] And all of this is simply to say in modern thought patterns what has been said long ago, namely that those who leave house or wife or children (a virginal life) for the kingdom "receive much more in the present time" as well as everlasting life in the age to come.[109] What could "much more" be if not a fuller enrichment in all that really matters?

Conclusion

It is now easy to see that one simply does not understand what a religious woman is unless he understands something of what the Church herself is and how the consecrated woman fits into God's people. We now find a deeper meaning in expressions of Vatican II relating religious to the mystery of the Church: special consecration deeply rooted in baptismal consecration,[110] a more intimate consecration in the Church,[111] living the life of the Church in a particular way,[112] belonging to the diocesan family in a special manner,[113] a special joining to the Church,[114] inseparable union with the life and holiness of the Church,[115] adornment of the Church,[116] symbol and witness to the world of Christian and ecclesial reality.[117] The reader will notice that the overriding emphasis in all this is what the sister *is,* not what she does. We have yet to consider the ecclesiality of the religious apostolate, an aspect of our subject that is so important we have devoted the following chapter to it. Yet all the same, our present discussion should make it clear that the basic ecclesiality of the religious woman derives from her existential, not her operational, reality.

CHAPTER TWO

FUNCTIONAL ECCLESIALITY
OF THE RELIGIOUS WOMAN

Incarnated reality is dual: matter-spirit, human-divine, visible-invisible. God has made a world. The Word has assumed flesh. The Father and the Son have sent their Spirit into man. As a consequence, man himself is immersed in a whole series of dualisms: individuality-sociality, being-acting, giving-receiving, knowing-willing, understanding-sensing, sacred-secular. But these dualisms are not dichotomies — they form unities, are blended finely and imperceptibly. The Church herself is dualistic in a remarkable unity: "It is of the essence of the Church that she be both human and divine; visible and yet invisibly endowed, eager to act and yet devoted to contemplation, present in this world and yet not at home in it." [1]

Because she is human and visible, the Church is structured. Because she is divine and invisibly endowed, she is charismatic. Both elements derive, not solely from a natural fittingness, but from the will of Christ. He who gave the binding and loosing power to Peter and the apostolic college also gave his own Spirit to dwell within the whole new people of his Father. He who commissioned a hierarchy so to teach in his name that those who hear them hear him and those who reject them reject him,[2] also sent his Spirit to teach "all things" and bring into the minds of his own all he himself had taught.[3] The structural-charismatic complementarity and tension inherent in the Temple-Church are present by divine intent. Though they raise problems, they should not surprise us.

The religious life poses several of these problems. How does it fit into the whole hierarchical structure of the Church? Is it solely charismatic? Does its own nature require a structure-charism dualism?

Charism

The religious life belongs to the charismatic, not the hierarchical element in the Church. What precisely is the charismatic? A charism is a Spirit-originated gift given to individuals of every rank for the benefit of the community, the people of God.[4] The Spirit originates charisms both ordinary and extraordinary, those that the world scarcely notices and those that no one can miss. We would call charismatic the skill of a spiritual director, zeal of a missionary, mercy of a nurse, devotion of a mother, burning contemplation of a Carmelite, writing of Augustine or Thomas, preaching of Chrysostom, journalism of Chesterton. Likewise charismatic are martyrdom, infallibility, virginity, poverty, miracles, tongues. These gifts are often new and unforeseen, for who can predict the Spirit, utter freedom? They are both institutional and non-institutional, those that belong to an office and those that do not. To distinguish between charism and office is to offer an inadequate (in the logical sense) and overlapping distinction, since one and the same Spirit endows the pope with infallibility, grants power to bishops and priests, graces the virgin with purity and the journalist with honesty. Non-institutional charisms are indispensable to the Church, because this Body of Christ is not only a hierarchical structure, but has also living within it the vivifying Spirit who moves all members to their tasks. Though these gifts derive from this Spirit, they are humanly guided by the hierarchy.[5] A harmony between the institutional and non-institutional charismata can be guaranteed only by the indwelling Spirit himself who originates both. In the case of a conflict only he can secure a suitable settlement, since there is no human authority outside the Church to whom one may appeal.[6]

The life of the evangelical counsels is a cluster of non-hierarchical charisms, for it pertains to the life of the Spirit, the holiness of the Temple of God. Virginity and poverty and obedience are given to the religious woman not only for her own fulfillment but also for the upbuilding of the whole people of God.

Structured and Unstructured Charisms

Does the religious community possess its own structure-charism dualism? Yes, it does. But we should notice that this question seems to suppose that structure and charism are adequately distinct. So perhaps one should ask: "Is a religious community gifted with both structured and unstructured charisms?" As we have indicated, the answer is affirmative. Since the Spirit is the first mover in the Church, the establishment of religious orders and their governing structures may be said to be his work. And those structures exist obviously for the good of the group. These juridical elements in a congregation are not hierarchical in the sense of having an immediately divine origin, but they are structural and derive immediately from the direction of the Church. We may say that papal-episcopal-sacerdotal structures are divine charisms, while religious governing structures are ecclesial charisms. Both derive from the Spirit, but differently.

Our questions, therefore, are answered in one sentence of Vatican II: "Although the religious state constituted by the profession of the evangelical counsels [7] does not belong to the hierarchical structure of the Church, nevertheless it belongs inseparably to her life and holiness." [8] Nor is the religious life a state somewhere between the lay and clerical states, since members of both these latter may be religious.[9] The precise place of religious lies in the "life and holiness" of the

Church, not in her jurisdictional structure. While some religious hold hierarchical offices, their primary function as religious is to witness to the life-giving Spirit, origin of sanctity. This is why Vatican II can also say that the *primary* reason religious are in a diocese is not their external apostolate, but rather prayer, penance and example of holiness.[10] This is why interior sanctity must hold "the leading role" in the promotion of apostolic renewal.[11] This is why the first witnessing task of religious is to remind the world of Christ in contemplation on the mountain.[12] Once again we may note that the sister who sees external apostolate as her first job does not understand the theology of her vocation. Her specific call is to the life of the Spirit. She may be called also to social work, or to nursing, or to teaching (and who would hesitate to proclaim the crucial need for these works?), but the fact remains that she is not first of all a worker. She is before all else concerned with the things of the Lord, how she may pray to him without distraction.[13]

The religious state belongs inseparably to the Church's life and holiness. This adverb, inseparably, seems to indicate that the religious life is so intricately bound up with what the people of God are about, so intimately tied-in with the gospel life that it shall be with us forever. Periodically, in the history of the Church, someone is likely to prophecy the death of religious life. Our day is no exception. Yet so closely bound up with evangelical perfection are consecrated virginity, voluntary poverty and ecclesial obedience, that to predict the disappearance of religious life is to assert the irrelevance of the gospel. The profession of the evangelical counsels may decline through human weakness, but disappear it will not.

That adverb, inseparably, relating religious to ecclesial holiness, suggests strongly that religious life cannot be secularized and remain religious. To state that in the congregations of the future spirituality will not hold the place of pre-eminence is to state a theological anomaly. This is not even good lay spirituality. For anyone in the Church, "action is directed and subordinated to contemplation" [14] with the consequence that no one may give his work the place of pre-eminence. History, both past and present, offers ample evidence that trends toward the secularization of the religious life do not terminate in half-way measures. They end with scandal and/or the very destruction of gospel holiness. The divine injunction, you cannot serve God and mammon, has been proven right more times than one can number. We can only hope that our 20th century religious will not prove it anew on a grand scale.

Charismatic Community

Individual religious possess individual charisms. To be persuaded of this fact we need only recall the individual gifts of Basil and Benedict, Dominic and Francis, Teresa and John, Francis and Jane. What congregation cannot point with justifiable pride not only to its founders but also to less known members as men or women with unique and beautiful gifts bestowed by the Spirit? Yet at the same time, we may speak, it seems, of a religious group as a charismatic plurality. We may think in terms of communal charisms, gifts given to a secondary group for the benefit both of that group and the primary group. The communal profession of genuine poverty profits not only the immediate community but the whole people of God in the local diocese and in the universal Church. This gift proclaims the primacy of God in his cosmos, the overriding necessity of his kingdom "superior to all earthly considerations," [15] the pilgrim situation of his people on earth, the freedom of Christ. It is a communal charism. The group profession of celibacy calls all the faithful to a more universal love, to more devoted service, to more faithful chastity, to deeper contemplation, to a more vivid awareness of the coming vision of the Lord in our risen bodies. It is likewise a communal charism.

Then there are, too, the more particularized charisms the Spirit has entrusted to individual religious congregations, charisms they have, not exclusively, but with a specialized emphasis: liturgical life and apostolate (Benedictines), teaching (Dominicans, Jesuits), nursuing (Charities, Mercies,) foreign missions (White Fathers, Maryknollers, Marist Missionary Sisters), contemplation (Carmelites, Poor Clares), poverty (Trappists, Little Brothers of Pere de Foucauld), passion of Christ (Passionists), Christian joy (Franciscans), devotion to God's Mother (Marian congregations). These are Spirit-originated gifts meant to enrich all the members of Christ's body. That they are ecclesial is obvious.

Mandated Apostolates

The Spirit moves not only to contemplation but also to action. The contribution of religious orders to the apostolic enterprise of the Church through the centuries can only be called vast. One cringes to imagine where the Church would be without the schools, colleges, parishes, hospitals, social services, missionary endeavors carried on by vowed men and women. Impressive, too, is the varied richness of manner in which Vatican II speaks of the apostolic dimensions of religious life. Religious enjoy a "firmer commitment" to the ministry of the Church [16] and they carry out this ministry in her name.[17] They make the Church "experienced" and "spend themselves increasingly" in their ministry of service.[18] Religious are associated in the work of redemption [19] as they implant, strengthen and extend the kingdom in every land.[20] Because the contemplative life "belongs to the fullness of the Church's presence," it is to be established everywhere.[21] This thoroughgoing ecclesiality in apostolate renders logical the conclusion that religious "live and think with the Church" as they "spend themselves completely on her mission." [22]

Yet we must search out still deeper roots, roots that are plunged into the very bosom of the Trinity. The new testament Trinity is an economic Trinity, a three-personed God who reveals his personal realities through what each person does in the world of men. The biblical account does not present Father, Son and Spirit living their own inner life without reference to salvation history. This is all the more remarkable when one recalls that this inner divine living depends in no least fashion on men or their universe. So it is that the Father, "origin without origin," is presented as creating the whole vast universe of men and things from nothing at all. His almighty saving power continually intervenes in the history of a selected people. He is forever a doing God. We learn from what he does that this originating Person abounds in power, wisdom, loving kindness. He is origin and first.

We learn, too, that he is origin of a Son who comes from him into the world as its salvation. This Son has all that the Father has. He alone knows the Father and makes him known to men. He speaks what he has heard from his Father, works as the Father works, gives life as the Father gives it. This Son is destined to a cross and is raised triumphantly from a tomb by his Father. And so we learn of the inner relations between Father and Son from their relations in man's salvation.

This Father and Son love each other with an unspeakable love, a love so unspeakable that in it, they breathe forth their whole nature into their common Bond-Kiss. We learn about this sanctifying Spirit because they send him into the world, and we understand from this sending that he proceeds from Father and Son in their inner relationship. We learn that he is the life-giving Spirit who makes holy and pours out love. We hear that he establishes ruling power in the Church, that he is the power to forgive sins, that he teaches all truth. We grow in our understanding of this Spirit, soul of the Church, by what he does in the Church.

Yes, the Trinity of revelation is a salvific, economic Trinity, and our apostolate finds its deepest roots in the silent bosom of a life that never began and shall never cease. All apostolate begins with the Origin without origin. "As the Father sent me, so am I sending you." [23] It is from the mission of the Son and the mission of the Holy Spirit that she (the Church) takes her origin, in accordance with the decree of God the Father." [24] And it is this same Church that sends each religious congregation into the vineyard of its Lord. Through the pontifical or episcopal approval of its fundamental document and by the acceptance of the community as such each institute is given an ecclesial status; it is sent. And it is sent anew each time it is given a new task by the local ordinary. Through her superiors each sister is likewise sent to her particular work, and so she finds herself in the third grade classroom or in a Newman center or in an operating room as an ecclesially mandated person. And all this began with the Father dwelling in her bosom. He begets his Son in an eternal begetting and sends him into the world of time incarnated in human flesh. This beloved Son establishes and sends his Church as he himself was sent. Within the eternal godhead Father and Son breathe forth their common Spirit and send him into the Church as its vivifying, unifying, sanctifying soul. The Church begets and gives life to the religious congregation and sends it to the faithful in her bosom. The congregation admits each sister into its inner family life and unity and sends her to a particular work. The sister is an ecclesial apostle. Her mission derives from the Father through the Son; it lives in the Spirit. She is a trinitarian apostle. She is anything but a purely private person.

Because the Church's apostolic mission is a social enterprise, a team effort, it demands a reasonably structured plan and execution. The simplest community activity requires basic structures at least: time, place, approach, goal. One is sociologically naive if he thinks a structureless apostolate possible, especially in a society that is growing into more complex and sophisticated organizational patterns, not lesser ones. This observation does not, of course, exclude either individual initiative or Spirit-originated freedom, but it does give both a context. We need, then, to inquire into the sisters' ecclesiality insofar as it touches upon her freedom and obedience within the Church at large and within her own institute.

Ecclesial Freedom

The individual Christified man is free, supremely free. He is free precisely to the extent that he is Christified. The fact that these two statements are far from obvious to every observer suggests that we explore them in some detail. Much loose talk about the freedom of God's sons stems from a confusion of differing kinds of freedom together with an altogether inadequate notion of what Scripture means by the specific type we are calling ecclesial or Spirit-originated freedom.

We may distinguish for our purposes, five kinds of human liberty. The most basic type is *psychological* freedom, a self-determining power given in man's very intellectual nature. Because he is spirit — incarnated, yes, but still spirit — man is opened to the unlimited in his knowing and loving. As spirit he bursts beyond the boundaries of the circumscribed particular and can be filled only by the universal truth, goodness, beauty. Hence, though he necessarily seeks to know, to love, to delight, he freely chooses the particular good he shall embrace. No finite created reality, not even the most beautiful human person, can fill and therefore necessitate his will. In all of his concrete choices man is his own self-determining master. Likewise flowing out of his intellectual nature is man's *moral* freedom. Supposing as it does psychological self-determination, this liberty involves an immunity from law, divine or human, civil or ecclesiastical. Thus, a man is morally free to kill in necessary self-defense but he is not free to murder. A third type of human liberty is *political* freedom, the power of a people to decide upon and regulate its own temporal destiny. This immunity from outside domination implies both psychological and moral freedoms. *Religious* freedom is the uncoerced living of one's religious beliefs in a pluralistic society. On the one hand, no man may be forced to act in a manner opposed to his religious tenets, and, on the other, he may not be prevented, within due limits, from acting in accord with those tenets.[25] Religious liberty is rooted both in man's personal, intellectual dignity and in the fact that his response to God's call must be self-determined.

Distinct from, but related to psychological, moral, political and religious freedoms is that of the son of God, Spirit-originated freedom, *the* freedom of man in the Church. This liberty supposes psychological self-determination but is something further that penetrates and elevates it, that raises it to a new plane, the plane of being supernaturally led by the Spirit. It implies two levels, both valid: a surface level according to which the new graced man is to be restricted by fewer external laws, and a deep level according to which something inner is done to this man in his deepest center.

We shall begin with the profound level, since it is the source of the consequences which lie on the surface of human, Christian life. Our first step in understanding this liberty of the son of God is to notice that in the old dispensation Yahweh had promised a new, superior, inner way of getting his people to do his will —

> I shall give you a new heart, and put a new spirit in you; I shall remove the heart of stone from your bodies and give you a heart of flesh instead. I shall put my spirit in you, and make you keep my laws and sincerely respect my observances.[26]

This new inner spirit, this interior power is a new principle of operation. It is an internal origin prompting a man to carry out what the external command indicates. Paul identifies this promised power with the Holy Spirit himself. So revolutionary is this transformation from external law to internal power that Christian men have Christ's law written in their very flesh: "It is plain that you are a letter from Christ, drawn up by us, and written not with ink but with the Spirit of the living God, not on stone tablets, but on the tablets of your living hearts." [27]

Our second step: this indwelling Spirit moving man to good from within is himself a law,[28] a superior kind of law, no doubt, but nonetheless a law. How can this be? Is not law associated with written formulation and forced compliance? How could the purest Spirit be a law? The problem readily dissolves when we recall the dual function of even human law, written law: informing, moving. An ecclesiastical or civil statute instructs the intellect regarding something to be done or omitted. A sign posted at the side of the freeway informs the driver of a speed limit. The statute via the sign also moves the will to observance through the coercive power of the state. In a superior manner, the indwelling Spirit teaches men "all things" and brings to their minds all that Christ had taught.[29] Like any law, he informs . . . but from within. He also moves the will to observance, but without forcing it. "It is God," says Paul, "who puts both the will and the action into you." [30] Because every good and perfect gift is given by the Father of lights,[31] all of a man's goodness — thought, desire, will, execution — is given from within. Indeed, the Spirit does all that a law does . . . and more. He is a law in a new and elevated sense.

Yet, paradoxically (and this is our third step), this law liberates. Ordinarily, we feel that statutes and commands limit us, hem us in. And so they do, but only to afford the individual and the group a wider scope for freedom, for being fully human. "Where the Spirit of the Lord is, there is freedom." [32] And the apostle can even say "if you are led by the Spirit, no law can touch you." [33] It would appear from these texts that a Spirit-led, directed society would be forced by no written law, for this society is free, can be touched by no statute. This sounds anarchic, chaotic. Yet this is precisely the condition of God's people: the Spirit-law frees them. How can they enjoy freedom and yet avoid chaos? Scripture commentators following St. Thomas explain Gal 5:18 by distinguishing two ways of being subject to a law: a) being obliged, and b) being coerced by it. All men, they point out, are obliged by the written law of Christ (as also by ecclesiastical and civil laws). Some men are

not coerced because, moved by the indwelling Spirit, they
spontaneously fulfill the written command because they want
to. They are liberated from the heavy hand of force, penalty,
fear, surveillance. They are free men living like mature adults.
The honest man liberated by the Spirit of truth is not subject
to the slavery of the consequences of lying: degradation, fear
of being found out, punished, despised. The chaste man is
no slave to the insatiable, burning desires of his flesh; he does
not get tangled in illicit affairs; he enjoys the honor of integrity
and the peace of virtue. He is free of the law because he is
moved by the Law, the Spirit. This is why the saint rejoices
in the Lord always: he is always doing what he wants to do
and he is always wanting what he does (and is not this wanting
what we do at the very heart of freedom?). This is why the
sinner is inveterately miserable: he is forever being forced to
do what he hates and repeatedly he does not want what he
does. The one is a free man, the other a slave.

Our fifth step: the crucial norm of Spirit-originated freedom
is love, love which necessarily brings with itself all good. Even
on the merely human plane a man who deeply loves another
gladly fulfills his duties toward that other, and more than his
duties. So also on the divine plane the love poured out in our
hearts by the Holy Spirit makes a man to be patient and kind,
to believe all things, to hope for all things, to endure all things.
It prompts him to flee envy, pretentiousness, self-seeking,
wickedness.[34] If he walks in the Spirit, he does not fulfill worldly
desires. Rather, he enjoys the fruits of the Spirit: joy, peace,
patience, purity, goodness.[35] Love is law.

Such is the freedom of the son of God. We would call it
the freedom of goodness. Most of us envision liberty to be an
immunity from force, restriction, necessity, and we are correct,
except for the fact that we assume this immunity to be the
prime factor, whereas it is secondary. Liberty is first of all for
something, not against something. If at this moment I am not
free to play the violin, the problem is not that someone is
holding me back, but rather that I do not possess the ensemble

of qualities (knowledge, motor skills, practice), the goodnesses that would enable me to perform. Freedom is a self-determining *power* to be or to do. I am not free to be or to act as a lawyer, physicist, surgeon, priest, unless I first possess the needed powers (knowledge, skills, authorization). Immunity from restriction is surely involved here, but it supposes and follows after the positive powers. And even restrictions are primarily for, not against. If a family backyard perched on a cliff is circled by a sturdy fence, the restriction is aimed at freeing the children to remain children. If they jump the fence, they are no longer free to be children, but only corpses.

So also with Spirit-originated freedom. It involves restrictions, of course: the "thou shalt nots." It implies immunities to be sure: immunity from the slavery to sin (pride, lust, avarice) and immunity from the darkness of error and ignorance.[36] All of this, however, is aimed at an interiorized, spontaneous, spirited impulse toward the full actualization of humanness, and that can only be a Christified humanness. Spirit-originated freedom is a new power to be *fully* human, and this "to be" is brought about by a whole series of new self-determinations that would be impossible were they not poured out by the Spirit who is given to us. A man freely moved by this inner Law whose norm is love is now free to become and act as a new man, fully a new man, so fully that he is now living a life that shall blossom into the unimaginable enthrallment of the beatific vision in a risen body.

Rightly understood, therefore, the freedom of the son of God is no threat to an integral Christian life. It is no capitulation to anarchy, to gay-blade living. Paul, intrepid proclaimer of freedom, sees no difficulty about submitting himself to the "men of authority" in Jerusalem,[37] and he repeatedly demands in his turn an entire obedience to his teaching and decisions. For the apostle the Christian is freed precisely by his austerity: possessing nothing,[38] content to be without superfluities,[39] preaching only a cross,[40] rejoicing in appalling sufferings.[41] To understand that Spirit-originated freedom is a resurrection-through-death freedom, we need only recall that love is its basic norm and that a love morality is maximal. Whereas a legal morality demands the least of a group (positive laws typically require the minimum), a love ethic requires the most. This is why the great commandment must have no limit: whole heart, whole soul, whole mind. This is why in order to have Christ a man must renounce all he possesses.[42] This freedom demands a complete openness. It demands everything in order to bestow everything.

Because this new Christ-liberty is the dignity of the people of God, it is an ecclesial liberty. The Spirit dwells in this people, and where the Spirit of the Lord is, there is freedom.[43] Freedom in the Church, therefore, is something more than psychological freedom. While the first supposes the second, it goes far beyond it. The Church is the home of freedom because it is the home of the Spirit. This is why authoritarianism, undue restrictions, petty red tape are so tragic, so unfortunate among God's people. This community is a free community because the Spirit lives in it.

Religious Woman: Free Woman

The virgin is a virgin in order to be free: "I would like to see you free from all worry." [44] So begins St. Paul's doctrine of consecrated virginity. He wants this woman to be completely free for the Lord and his concerns. She is the ideal image of ecclesial freedom, for she is virgin temple of the Spirit. Her whole way of life is aimed at liberty and her all-encompassing law is love. Her virginal poverty and obedience open her to a keen sensitivity to the Spirit-origin of all freedom among the sons of God, his people. She is universal lover made fruitful by the overshadowing of the Holy Spirit. We may view the sister as model of ecclesial freedom by studying its traits in her.

Self-direction from within. The son of God has interiorized the gospel; he has the law of his God in his heart.[45] Because he walks by the Spirit, he does not fulfill the lusts of the flesh.[46] He does what he ought to do not because of external pressures or threats of punishment but because he himself is a letter of Christ, because the Spirit of the living God has written the Christ law on his very heart.[47] As we have considered in our first chapter, the consecrated virgin is a special temple of the indwelling Spirit. As such she has this inner Law deeply implanted in her innermost person center. She has interiorized the gospel not only by continual meditation on it but also by the direct enlightenment of him whom the Father has sent to teach all things and brings to her mind all that the Son has taught.[48] Because her whole evangelical way of life is orientated to an intimacy with him, she is especially fitted to enjoy what he brings: joy, peace, love, goodness, gentleness, self-control.[49] Led by this inabiding Spirit she freely originates from her profound center all that the gospel law says. She is self-directed from within.

Maturity in obedience. The term, immaturity, has become in contemporary religious jargon a much-abused term. If one does not like an approach or a practice, he need only call it immature and that is supposed to settle the matter in his favor. For this reason we dislike calling our second trait of the free man maturity in obedience. Yet we must use the word because it is not here taken as a mere label of approval but as saying exactly what we wish to say. It is typical of a child's obedience that he complies with a regulation out of extrinsic reward-punishment motivation. This is good, but rudimentary, incomplete. It should be typical of an adult's obedience that he follows out a directive because he sees and wills the intrinsic goodnesses of the obedience itself and the value of the activity commanded. We note this maturity in the psalmist: "Your commandments fill me with delight, I love them deeply ... Meditating all day on your Law, how I have come to love it!" [50] This man loves and enjoys both the fact that God commands and the very goodness of what he commands. This man is spiritually grown up. He is mature. Because the *raison d'etre* of the virgin is that she love with an undivided heart and be wholly concerned with the affairs of the Lord, the more she attains the purpose of her consecration, the more mature and free she is in her obedience. She should be to the whole Church a model of one so in love with her Lord that his least desire is her entire will.

Peace in obedience. Any man can be disturbed and annoyed by an unreasonable regulation, but only the imperfect man is much bothered by just directives. Because the latter is swayed by and subject to unruly impulses, he finds himself continually inclining to unreasonable activities, and so, as St. Paul says, laws are made not for the just but for the unjust and rebellious[51] — they are made for slaves. The saint on the other hand is already freely moved by the indwelling Spirit to want what the law indicates, and so he does not need it, is not annoyed by it, not a slave to it. "Universal peace for those who love your law, no stumbling block for them." [52] Since religious life is a school of evangelical holiness, it is a school of freedom and peace. The sister's early formation, her contemplation and spiritual reading, the asceticism of her vows and the warmth of her human love, all these slowly interiorize the gospel in her heart. If she lives this life fully, she is not annoyed by a rule of silence (library or convent), she does not rebel against the magisterium when loyalty demands keen sacrifice, she does not chafe under the normal restrictions attendant on any community life. She enjoys a universal peace because she is free.

Freedom through obedience. It seems an outrageous assertion to say that obedience liberates a man. Yet this is precisely what both Sacred Scripture and ecclesiastical documents say. The psalmist can confidently assert that "having sought your precepts, I shall walk in all freedom," [53] while Vatican II can speak of religious obedience as strengthening liberty,[54] and as leading the human person to a maturity as a consequence of the enlarged freedom belonging to God's sons.[55] How can this be? How can a virtue which seems to diminish a man, to hem him in, to make him into a child actually mature him, set him free? The key to understanding this paradoxical situation is, we think, the remembrance that freedom is a positive power before it is anything else, an openness for before it is an immunity from. Human liberty is a self-determining energy for achieving human completeness. For the son of God human completeness can only be an entire Christification. So the question becomes: how does obedience open a man to a self-determining Christification? From the negative point of view, first of all, it generally preserves a man from mistakes that would diminish his ardent pursuit of the Lord. Is not this precisely the function of the restrictions in religious constitutions? In the same way the tracks restrict a train in order that it may function as a train — it could not run a tenth of a mile roaming through a soft field. Or, to change our image, just as the cliffside fence restricts a child from being a corpse but not from being a child at play, so do sensible regulations in convent life prevent a religious from being less a woman, not from being more. These limits liberate her to be completely an evangelical, ecclesial woman.

Obedience positively opens a man to Christification in several ways. It offers him the wisdom of another mind, often enough a less emotionally involved and therefore more objective mind. And do not truth and wisdom open a mind, enlarge it, free it? "You will learn the truth and the truth will make you free." [56] Secondly, obedience blends a man into his social group, fits him into community living. Since he is by nature social, whatever enables him to grow socially enables him to become more a man. His inner self-determining energy is given wider scope for operation. Who could deny that a girl by entering an ecclesial community (which itself in turn has entered the diocesan and worldwide ecclesial community) is opened in her obedience to far more universal social encounters and growth than she would have enjoyed in a limited, four-or-six member family? Thirdly, religious obedience frees the sister for a universal apostolate to her neighbor. Not only is she opened for her own personal growth to wider social encounters, she is also given opportunity for a universal and maternal love. This is one of the most plain, most tangible liberties involved in the vow of obedience. *If she is the kind of person she ought to be* (*loving, affectionate, prayerful*), the sister loves warmly far more men, women and children than would have been possible in the married state. And conversely (supposing the same condition), she will receive more love in her virginal consecration than she would have received in marriage. Though these statements may seem to be mere pious exaggerations, we invite an objector to consider our condition carefully and to investigate current experimental studies on happiness in marriage. Lastly, obedience liberates because it is part and parcel of the concrete, existential divine economy in which real men live. Abstract men of pure nature may have operated otherwise. But there is no such thing as even one abstract man of pure nature. What God has a matter of fact done is to set real men in an obediential economy. Salvation history is interwoven with divinely authorized men who are to act in the name of Yahweh and direct others according to his will. We meet the Lord, of course, in a direct prayer communion, but we also meet him in other men. Obedience to divinely authorized men is an encounter with God himself: "You must all obey the governing authorities. Since all government comes from God, the civil authorities were appointed by God, and so anyone who resists authority is rebelling against God's decision." [57] Here in the thought of Paul the divine origin of authority could hardly be put more plainly, and, indeed, it is also plain in Peter: "For the sake of the Lord, accept the authority of every social institution." [58] Now, if we meet God himself in obedience, we are opened by obedience, for God is the good of every man. As plants are opened by contact with the sun and turn to the sun as their good, so we are brought to a human fullness by being turned to the Father in obedience to men. And human fullness implies freedom. Because the sister lives a life penetrated with ecclesial freedom-through-obedience, she is once again a witness to the strength and maturity the son of God should enjoy in the existential economy of the pilgrim Church. As obedient she is ecclesial and free.

Initiative in freedom. Unexpected though it may be in view of our immediately preceding remarks, the son of God learns to combine obedience with spontaneous initiative. The theology of Spirit-originated liberty simply demands it. If the Holy Spirit really leads and thus liberates a man from within, Church structures must provide for men responding to his inner, immediate impulses. The unique individual must initiate movement, if he is moved by the indwelling Spirit. He (the man) cannot always wait for an order from human superiors. The dynamic element in the Church is as much an element in her nature as is the structural. The love of Christ drives the Christian on,[59] and he must be driven. He has a duty to respond. He has a duty to initiate. Vatican Council II recalled this theological fact more than once. We are told, on the one hand, that the Holy Spirit is "impelling the Church to open new avenues of approach to the world of today," [60] and on the other that obedience leads to a "more mature freedom" and demands that priests "lovingly and prudently look for new avenues" while remaining ready to submit to the judgment of due authority.[61] If the Spirit impels to newness, man must initiate newness. This offers a further reason why religious must look for new forms, new solutions to their structural-charismatic problems. Pat, either/or solutions are inadequate. They are too simple, even naive. We need the both/and answer, charism and structure, freedom and obedience, initiative and regulation.

Consequences of Ecclesial Freedom for Formation

If the religious life is a witness to the Church as home of liberty we must find in it an increasingly clearer delineation of the delicate balance between Spirit-originated freedom and Spirit-authorized hierarchy.[62] The religious woman should show how she has interiorized the gospel, why

3

she obeys because she wants to obey, why just regulations do not disturb her, how her obedience frees her and sparks her initiative to act.

This ecclesial freedom begins in the formation of the young woman from the first day she affiliates herself with the congregation. The aim of that formation cannot be a mere external conformity, even a perfect external conformity. The whole thrust of the program must be to bring the candidate to what we have called the mature freedom of goodness. Some external conformity, of course — what societal group could survive without it? But none for its own sake, none that does not serve the person and the group, none that destroys spontaneity. The new religious woman must do what is right chiefly because she is sensitive enough to the indwelling Spirit to see and want what is right.

Furthermore, formation must be love penetrated, for love is the crucial norm of the son of God. If this observation is more than a rosy platitude, what does it mean? It means that love is the first rule young candidates learn. And what does this imply? It does not imply, as should be abundantly clear from all we have said, that religious women may do as they please, provided they "love". . . for the very good reason that this "love" is not love at all. Love as first rule of the convent implies exactly what it implies on the lips of Jesus when he speaks it as the great commandment for all men. It implies that young candidates learn early and thoroughly that they are in the convent for one reason, that "they seek God before all things and only Him," [63] and that this love is lived in a deep communion — contemplation of him joined to a warm, serving love of men. Love penetration in formation means that all other rules are related and subordinated to this one thing necessary. It reflects the Petrine idea that love comes before all else:[64] before ladylike posture, manners, gait; before specific practices and customs. Surely we are not belittling feminine proprieties and reasonable practices. They are necessary. But they are not first. Love is. This primacy of love implies like-

wise that all else be inspirited with love: that gait be related
to love as also setting a table properly and making one's bed,
and observing silence.

Love penetration of sister education means, furthermore,
that a maximal spirituality be taught to these young women.
They want it . . . when they arrive. If later their sights drop
to something less, that is most likely due either to diluted
teaching or to apostles of mediocrity, or to both. But there
is a still deeper reason why formation must be maximal: Christianity is maximal from top to toe. Overpowering in both
testaments is the omnipresent vehemence and totality of man's
pursuit of the Lord Yahweh: "I have sought you with *all* my
heart . . . You must love the Lord your God with all your
heart . . . You must therefore be perfect just as your heavenly
Father is perfect." [65] Who could ask more? May formation
ask less? True enough, a maximal morality does not always
ask everything at once. It does not break the reed or smother
the smoldering flax, but it never suggests that less than all will
be enough. Though it gently urges to the heights, it does not
rush the Holy Spirit. Though it teaches the full gospel, it adapts
practices to current strength. Love is dynamic. It grows.

Consequences of Ecclesial Freedom for Religious Rules

The human dignity of a man demands
that he be free to determine his own way to fulfillment within
the context of his own nature, divine law and the good of others.
He may not be submitted to another human person without
good reason, for he cannot develop into a full individual if he
is psychologically blocked by unreasonable fears, ignorance,
restrictions. Yet he still needs regulations because he is imperfect. Laws not only promote the common good; they also
form the individual person. What, then, does Spirit-originated
freedom mean for religious women who have chosen explicitly
to live a life that has for centuries been highly structured and

regulated? Does it mean that rules must go, or only some of them?

The ordinary sister would be the last to claim that she is perfect, and so she would also be the last to feel no need of continual guidance in her pursuit of the Lord. Though she is working to enflesh the gospel law in her heart, as a pilgrim she still needs an external map and companion assistance. Yet because she also has the Spirit abiding in her heart teaching and enlightening, her external map and companion assistance may not shackle this Spirit. Her rules ought to be necessary ones, necessary to insure a full gospel life, but they should be neither too many nor too specific. The sister should normally decide for herself what any adult woman decides. If poverty or the common good or ordinary courtesy require permission or notification, this she does. Hence, a religious abuses the liberty of God's children when in its name she takes the convent car out for the evening and tells no one. A courteous wife (or husband) would not think of so acting. She is not abusing this freedom when she decides which doctor she shall consult, what workshop she would like to attend, what time she shall retire for the evening.

Ecclesial freedom means that the sister is allowed to be herself naturally and supernaturally. She and the community need to learn to live the delicate balance between commonness and uniqueness. Because we share traits in common — intellect, will, emotions, aspirations — we humans share and act in common. We attend lectures, read books, participate in seminars, dine, play and worship together. Because each of us is unique, irrepeatable, we add, subtract, modify in our common sharings.

Though uniqueness is a priceless gift, what we have together is far more important than what we have separately. That I can think at all is infinitely more significant than that I have my own peculiar twists in thinking. Chesterton has remarked that "death is more tragic even than death by starvation. Having a nose is more comic even than having a Norman nose." [66]

A religious woman agrees to a whole list of commonnesses when she enters a religious congregation. They are indicated in the community's basic document and she may not excuse herself from them on a frivolous plea of being a free person. Yet at the same time this basic document and her fellow religious must respect her uniqueness and its reasonable expression.

One needs only half an eye to see that this area of freedom and obedience is crucial for the success of long-term renewal endeavors. Irresponsible abuses of liberty invite the pendulum to swing back to rigid authoritarianism and/or to the chaotic dissolution of a once-effective congregation. Unfortunately, we have difficulty in learning from history.

Freedom and Contemplation

Because the Spirit operates more effectively from within than man-made rules do from without, we can understand easily enough that the best way to secure obedience in the Church (as in the convent) is to deepen prayer communion with our indwelling God. A man sensitive to the inner light and promptings of the Holy Spirit freely and gladly does what he ought to do. This is not only good theory, it is good practice. A prayerful person is no threat to a just regulation, no pain to her superior. She knows from her intimacy with her Beloved what the consecrated virgin ought to be doing. And she does it.

Ecclesial Obedience

Freedom is prior to obedience. Yet freedom is protected and furthered by obedience. This we have just considered. It remains for us to investigate how the obedience of the religious woman is an ecclesial obedience. Does this vow, too, make her to be a woman of the Church in some manner over and above that of her married sister? It seems to us that there are three ecclesial roots to religious obedience:

community, school of gospel sanctity, apostolate. We shall consider each in turn.

Ecclesial community. A religious institute is a group of women who have determined to live the gospel totally and in community: they live the whole evangelical life as virgins, as poor, as serving, as contemplative, as worshiping. They are in miniature and intensely what the whole people of God is to be before Yahweh, our Father. They are called together in the name of and for the universal community, though they live in a local community. Sisters, therefore, are far more than a pious group of women, a Catholic club.

Now community demands structure. One is innocent of the facts of sociology if he thinks men can build a social group, including a Christian group, without at least a minimal place for organization, authority, directives and obedience. It is ironical that in an age in which civil society is trying to solve the problems inherent in the growing complexity of modern life by a growing specialization and sophistication, some in religious society are pushing in an opposite direction. This opposite push is quite correct in some areas (this we have supported above in our discussion of Spirit-originated freedom) but it is naive in others. Surely it is odd to see a religious woman demand liberties (e.g., leaving the convent at night without notifying anyone) that no business woman, no married woman would expect at the office or in the home. Even common courtesies are a form of structure.

Yet, authority exists for community, not community for authority. This is so true that Christian authority is a servant to the community. The Christian superior washes the feet of his subjects, he is humble, does not lord it over his own as do the pagans. When he commands (as he sometimes has the duty to command), he acts to serve the brethren. In important matters, he consults first and usually follows the consensus that may develop, but he does not shirk his responsibility to decide and implement. Community demands leadership, decision, even correction. And it demands obedience as well. Religious authority emerges from ecclesial community.[67] Obedience does likewise.

School of gospel sanctity. Religious life is an intense process of total Christification. To use the expressions of St. Paul, it is a becoming of true images of the Son, being members of Christ Jesus, living the life of Jesus, Christ living in a man, being clothed in him, belonging to him, becoming the perfect Man, becoming fully mature with Christ's fullness, growing into Christ, a living which *is* Christ.[68] The religious woman adds to the layman's pursuit of this Christification a specific way of life designed to reduce impediments, to facilitate the pursuit. This way of life is therefore a school, for who can know this specific way of the counsels unless he be taught? The living of this life, implies a continual learning of this life. It implies instruction, yes, but more than instruction. It implies biblically inspired leadership and direction, both written and spoken. It implies a student who learns and obeys.

Apostolate. Religious apostolate is plainly ecclesial. The saving Son did not commission his continuing work to any but the Church. So true is this that he who hears the Church hears him and he who rejects the Church rejects him and the Father who sent him.[69] The need for authority-obedience in the apostolic work carried on by religious can be shown by several considerations. First of all, the communality itself of apostolic endeavor demands a coordinating and directing principle. A team without direction is chaos. Business understands this so well that some religious by comparison appear naive in their expectations of unrestricted freedom.

Secondly, religious are not private persons in their work but rather ecclesially mandated persons. As such, they and their work are guided by the Church that sent them. Finally, the charismatic element in the sister's apostolate lies subject to the same testing as do other charisms. She is no exception. Indeed, the Spirit working in her should not be extinguished, but nonetheless, her gifts need to be tested.[70] She, too, must live her Spirit-originated freedom within the context of obedience.

The obedience of the religious woman is, therefore, thoroughly ecclesial, and in manners not shared by the married woman. This vow does indeed make her to be a woman of the Church in several manners over and above the lay way of life. It likewise enables her to share more deeply in the redemptive power of Christ's own obedience to the death on a cross.[71]

Even though this evangelical counsel is not as clearly taught in the New Testament as are virginity and poverty, these few remarks on the ecclesiality of religious obedience do show how necessarily implied it is. If the Christian virgin is to live and pray and work in communion with other virgins, she will necessarily be obedient in her new freedom.

Church of Alleluia

The Church is the home of joy just as it is the home of freedom. Augustine could say that the Christian should be an alleluia from head to foot. And he is such neither by accident nor by idle triumphalist boast but by the simple fact that he is a living stone of the spiritual house that is home to purest Joy.

Scripture of both testaments is replete with clapping hands, shouting forests, dancing maidens. The Temple-Church is an alleluia Church because Joy dwells within her. "There is a river whose streams refresh the city of God, and it sanctifies the dwelling of the Most High. God is inside the city," [72] a holy mountain "beautiful where it rises, joy of the whole world." [73] Those who take refuge in the Lord exult with endless shouts of joy,[74] for he works wonders for those he loves [75] and they sing to him for the goodnesses he shows them.[76] Yahweh gladdens man with his very presence.[77] He can be tasted with an experience that causes a visible radiance of joy,[78] for he shines with a perfection of beauty.[79] Yahweh promises unbounded joy in his presence, everlasting pleasures,[80] a gazing to one's fill on his face.[81] And so this people of God drink of his delight, a river of pleasure;[82] they enjoy his sweetness in his temple.[83] Even the pursuit of the Lord is joy and gladness.[84] The man who yearns for him thrills with delight, his heart and his flesh "sing for joy to the living God." [85] This extraordinary joy of the godly man derives also from his very goodness as a man. Being rejoices in its own fullness: "Rejoice in Yahweh, exult, you virtuous, shout for joy, all upright hearts." [86] This is so because Yahweh's plan is a pleasure plan — it is the only plan for man that works.[87] He alone has done "astounding things in the world," for he is a worker of marvels.[88] The word of the Lord is itself a joy to the heart, sweeter than honey, more precious than the finest gold.[89] He is good, his love everlasting.[90] The man who lives by this word of love finds a new charm in created beauties, since "the very Author of beauty has created them." [91]

All of this helps to explain the omnipresence of alleluias in the missal and office texts. The liturgy is a song of the Church's joy: "Let us wake in the morning filled with your love and sing and be happy all our days,[92] . . . come, let us praise Yahweh joyfully [93] . . . burst into shouts of joy [94] . . . telling of his marvels [95] . . . what immense joy for us!" [96]

The New Testament looks upon the Church in the same light. Joannine literature speaks of the disciples' joy as full and complete.[97] Paul overflows with joy himself and admonishes others to rejoice in the Lord *always*.[98] Peter speaks of tasting the very sweetness of the God who dwells in the Church, a spiritual house.[99]

All of this may of course sound too good to be true. Unreal and exaggerated. Is it? Admittedly, there is no rosier picture of life in the universe. Yet no one may dismiss the idea unless he has first tried to play the game according to the plan. And play it fully. We can say without hesitation that the most happy people, radiantly happy people, permanently happy people, we have met on the face of this earth, are men and women who enjoy a profound intimacy with their indwelling God. This is a fact, and one cannot successfully argue with facts. In these people alone we find fulfilled the astonishing claims Scripture makes for those who dare to pursue the Lord God with an entire commitment and a deep prayer life. And this suggests a new facet to the ecclesiality of the consecrated virgin. The whole *raison d'etre* of her dedicated chastity is that she be "free from care," easily able to be concerned with the things of the Lord, undistracted in her prayer life.[100] The whole thrust of Catholic teaching through the centuries all the way from St. Paul through Vatican II is that the first reason a virgin is a virgin is loving contemplation of her inabiding Beloved.[101] If this indwelling Joy is the fountainhead of an unspeakable delight, if he gives himself, no less, to be tasted, surely she who has left all else to obtain a hundredfold even in this life [102] is an alleluia par excellence. She has somehow left the world to attain the "joy of the whole world." [103] She especially has taken refuge in the Lord and so should shout with living, thrilling joy. If the person who yearns for the Lord thrills with delight, she of all persons should "sing for joy to the living God." [104] She most unqualifiedly can say: "I look to no one else in heaven, I delight in nothing else on earth. My flesh and my heart are pining with love . . . My joy lies in being close to God." [105] If the Church is an alleluia Church, the religious woman is its most obvious alleluia. Those who know the inner spiritual life of very many sisters know that this is not only good theory. It is fact. It is a simple reflection of the first consecrated virgin who said of herself, "My spirit exults in my Savior." [106]

Mary, Charismatic Model

Among all unique events in the ages of cosmic history the supremely unique is the incarnation. And since there can be no human birth without a human mother, there can be no birth of Christ without the Mother of Christ.

Mary is *the* unique among women. She is *the* ecclesial woman. Though we have not continually pointed it out, one can easily see how this loveliest of women fits into almost every nook of this volume as the complete exemplification of what we have been about: transcendence of God and his immanence, sacred woman, temple of the Spirit, sacrament of salvation, virgin, mother, pilgrim, ecclesial freedom and obedience. What the sister is, Mary is — first and foremost.

We should like at this point to notice a little more closely how the Mother of God is the pattern for our understanding of the ecclesiality of the religious woman. The first and overwhelming truth about Mary is that her whole being exists for Christ and Christ alone. He is her *raison d'etre*. He is center, end and all. The same is true of the religious woman: she is consecrated by vow for no other than Christ. He is her *raison d'etre* as a religious — another reason she is not first of all a teacher or nurse or social worker. The virgin is concerned about the things of the Lord, how she may pray without distraction.[107]

Mary is mother through and through. She was tailor-made by the Father for the incarnation of his Son. She was tailor-made for motherhood from the first moment of her conception, a stainless conception. She is mother of the whole Christ, head and members. The sister sees in this Virgin a model of motherliness to imitate: life-givingness, warmth, concern. Every healthy woman yearns to be fruitful, to communicate and foster life. Mary bore the Author of life, who is life itself.

Mary is virgin, the purest, loveliest virgin. With her a consecrated and complete purity began. The Church's virginity began with her, as does the sister's. In this Mother of God, the Church is already perfect and without stain.[108] More than any other she says for the Church and for the sister, " I look to no one else in heaven, I delight in nothing else on earth. My flesh and my heart are pining with love ... My joy lies in being close to God." [109] She is virgin centered on Christ.

Mary is temple of the Spirit. She is the woman who is overshadowed by the Spirit, made immaculate and fruitful by him, raised gloriously into heaven by him. One of the most telling traits of the covenant betwen Yahweh and his people was his selection of this nation as *his* nation and his consequent presence among them. It was a mysterious presence but it was real, real with the reality of electricity. The new dispensation brought the revelation of splendid new dimensions to this presence: tri-personal and indwelling. The place of this presence was the new people of God, the Church. And Mary was the beginning of it all and its perfect exemplification. If the religious woman has a special relevance to the indwelling mystery, the virgin Mother of God is prime analogate. She is temple without stain, temple of joy, temple of contemplation, temple of burning love.

Mary did not belong to the structural hierarchical element in the Church but to the charismatic. Her gifts were the inner life-giving gifts of the Spirit possessed in an entirely unique manner and degree. She was thoroughly charismatic, docile and sensitive to this Spirit who was her law from within. How could one make exterior regulations for the first consecrated virgin? How does one legislate in human words for a Mother of God? How could a man formulate norms for one who had been untouched by the primal sin? She was utterly led by the Spirit. She is the shining exemplar of the ecclesial woman, a woman so sensitive to the breathing of the soul-Spirit of the Church that she is always to the people of God a light and a love, a picture in the flesh of what a Christ life looks like.

And such is the way this Virgin exercises her queenly power. She rules not as a man, but as a woman. She governs not by passing laws, issuing orders, handing down decisions, but by living, loving, praying. She is every bit a woman of the Church but not operating as her Son. The sister is every bit a woman of the Church, but not operating as a priest. She is feminine and should glory in the fact. Just as Mary was needed in the incarnation with all her womanly beauties and gifts, so is the sister needed in the Church with each of her feminine graces and qualities. The religious needs to become more a woman, not less. To do this she cannot do better than to gaze upon the perfect Woman.

Jesus' Mother is image of Jesus' poverty and obedience. She shared them and lived them from the moment of her fiat in the presence of Gabriel to the moment of her acquiescence on Calvary. Volumes are filled with reflections on the poverty and obedience found in the family of Nazareth; we need not add to them here. We may note, however, that the pilgrim Church still needs evangelical women to teach by their lives that a humble obedience to men is as precious to the eyes of God in the twentieth century as it was in the first. The pilgrim Church still needs virgins to shout that bodily beauty, extensive wardrobes, fine jewelry lie on the surface of reality. The Church needs woman who plainly live the ideal of Peter: "Do not dress up for show: doing up your hair, wearing gold bracelets and fine clothes; all this should be inside, in a person's heart, imperishable: the ornament of a sweet and gentle disposition — this is what is precious in the sight of God. That was how the holy women of the past dressed themselves attractively." [110] Where can the sister find a better picture of genuine feminine beauty than in the Virgin Mother? Where else *the* ecclesial Woman?

Mary is model of the ecclesial mystery in its final bloom. Living gloriously in her risen body, enthralled with a direct vision of her tri-personal God, this Virgin is now experiencing the eternal fullness of the Church. She is enthralled with what eye has not seen, nor ear heard, nor what the wildest fancy of human imagination could conceive. She is radiant in what awaits those who love God: tasting and seeing how good he is. This Virgin is now in completion, reality, vision what the religious virgin is in pilgrimage, sign, faith. She is the King's Mother radiant in final, ever-living, beauty. She is the beacon to the religious woman, ecclesial woman.

CHAPTER THREE

ECCLESIAL WOMEN: IMPLICATIONS

Theology aims at life. And good theory makes for good practice or it is not good theory. Our outline of the ecclesiality of the religious woman should yield a sound, progressive, thoroughly Catholic spirituality for the modern religious woman. At this point in our study it is now clear that the sister is an ecclesial woman or she is nothing. Perhaps there could have been some non-ecclesial, communal consecration in another supernatural economy, but in the economy in which we do as a matter of fact live there is no other way to be a religious woman in full Christian community than to be an ecclesial woman.

This theological truth must have relevance for real life. Indications of this relevance we have suggested here and there in our first two chapters. It remains for us now to underline these indications and to add to them.

Change and Stability

The Church is both stable and mutable because she is dual: incarnational and eschatological, "both human and divine, visible and yet invisibly endowed, eager to act and yet devoted to contemplation, present in this world and yet not at home in it." [1] She is stable because she is divine, invisibly gifted, deeply contemplative, ordained to the eternal. She is mutable because she is human, visible, acting, present in a changing world. She brings out of her storeroom things both old and new,[2] a permanent heritage and a fresh creativity, faithful to the one, open to the other. She changes within a stability because her progress is really change, not annihilation, for change implies a core reality perduring through transformations, while annihilation bespeaks utter destruction, and utter creation with nothing perduring.

The Church changes. So do religious women. They are ecclesial. What changes and what remains forever? The human changes as also do the visible, the acting, the presence to this world. Because they are of human origin, most structures in convent life are subject to modification. Rules suitable to one time and place may or may not be suitable to another. The same we may say of many, but not all, of the insights of a congregation's foundress. The cultural traits of a given nation, the customs of a community are obviously susceptible to alteration. Forms expressing gospel poverty and obedience may vary to some extent. Though their inherent orientation is fixed, the manner of implementation is not. This is why religious institutes may experiment with new democratic forms of government, forms that are not only compatible with the evangelical life but perhaps even more conducive to it. To take seriously the opinion of the youngest sister, for example, sounds akin to the last being first. Apostolic approaches are also subject to evolving progress. Reading the signs of the times, being vibrantly present to a constantly changing world not only permit but demand corresponding changes in approach to this world. In all these ways the householder draws out new things from his storeroom.

But he also retains old things, old things that are always new, the divine and the invisible. These are old only in the sense that they are timeless, always new. Stable realities are forever fresh. Man wrinkles in body but not in soul. Just acts change, but not justice. Beauties disintegrate but beauty remains forever lovely. It is this sort of reality in the religious life that never loses its crispness, its validity. Contemplation of the Lord is forever central because he is forever the Lord and no one can ever drink him out. To gaze on him in loving embrace is always a new enthrallment. Religious are always and everywhere contemplative — this can never change. Silence and solitude share in the same timelessness, for they are conditions for gazing on the loveliness of the Lord. They are conditions for being human. Worship is indispensable. Forms of silence, solitude, contemplation, liturgy may change, but not the core realities. Essential, too, in the life of the religious woman is the ecclesial obedience of the poor virgin in community. The most radical changes in convent living must always leave the sister a pure virgin, a poor pilgrim, an obedient woman of the Church.

We may mention here a contribution to the people of God made by consecrated women that has not, to our knowledge, been adequately noticed. We refer to the development of our understanding of revelation, surely an ecclesial reality. To appreciate this facet of the sister's ecclesiality we must dip briefly into the theology of sacred tradition and its relation to divine revelation. In this strict sense tradition is the living, continuous presentation by the Church of the saving truth of Christ committed to the apostles. "Saving truth" here does not refer only to revealed propositions but also to saving events which include both deeds and words. "Living, continuous presentation" indicates the dynamism inherent in divine tradition. It is not a static series of statements issued once for all, never to be developed or improved. These words also suggest the unbroken oneness of the Church's twentieth century preaching with that of the first. "Presentation by the Church" is not to be understood as limited to the magisterium. All the people of God participate in preserving, living, declaring in word and in action the healing revelation of Christ. Papal encyclicals and conciliar documents surely are vehicles of sacred tradition but so also are the private prayer of the housewife, the reflective

study of the school boy, the celebration of parish liturgy. "What
was handed on by the apostles includes *everything* which contributes to the holiness of life, and the increase in faith of
the People of God; and so the Church, in her *teaching, life,*
and *worship,* perpetuates and hands on to all generations *all*
that she herself is, all that she believes." [3] The universal words,
"everything, all" do not, of course, canonize the erring preaching of an undereducated priest or the mistaken prayer of a
layman — they refer to the Church's authentic, substantial life.

We are now prepared to understand the functions of the
religious woman a propos of sacred tradition. These functions
are threefold. First of all she lives the saving message totally.
The consecrated virgin incarnates the whole gospel in her flesh.
She is a woman of faith who lives in her body not only the
commandments but also the counsels. She incarnates the creed
in her person and proclaims it to the world by her life. Secondly,
in her intimate contemplative encounter with her indwelling
God she experiences what the divine realities mean, she (and
the Church, consequently) grows in understanding the divine
self-disclosure. The Spirit is bringing to her mind what Christ
Jesus has taught. [4] In a remarkable passage dealing with the
Church's growth in understanding divine revelation Vatican
II names, not theologians' tractates, but the faithfuls' contemplation and study. "There is a growth in the understanding of
the realities and the words which have been handed down. This
happens through the contemplation and study made by believers,
who treasure these things in their hearts (cf. Lk 2:19, 51),
through the intimate understanding of spiritual things they
experience." [5] Through the virgin concerned with the affairs
of the Lord, praying to him without distraction, [6] the Church
is growing in understanding her Lord. Through this virgin's
contemplative experience the Church is tasting her Lord and
seeing how good he is. [7] Thirdly, she formally teaches the word
in her apostolate. Her nursing, teaching, counseling are works
of love and truth performed in the name of the Church. She
is a living part of the living Christ transmitting the truths and

realities of saving history to all men. She contributes to ecclesial
tradition.

Love for the Church

"A man possesses the Holy Spirit to
the measure of his love for Christ's Church." [8] If the sister
is an ecclesial woman, she loves the Church. If her whole
being is penetrated with all the ecclesiality we have considered,
it is unthinkable that she is anything other than a woman deeply
in love with the People of the Father, the Body of Christ, the
Temple of the Spirit. She is so utterly in love with Christ that
she unreservedly loves what is his. And he has identified this
Church with himself in terms that could not be more plain:
"Anyone who listens to you, listens to me; anyone who rejects
you, rejects me." [9] The genuine religious woman listens to the
Church, is taught by the Church, accepts the Church, all because she loves and accepts Christ.

The sister loves the Church because the Holy Spirit is the
soul of this Body, a soul that makes this Church divine, just
as a man's soul makes matter human. This Spirit-presence in
the Temple Church makes her precious, so precious that St.
Paul does not hesitate to threaten divine vengeance on anyone
who harms her: "Didn't you realize that you were God's temple
and that the Spirit of God was living among you? If anybody
should destroy the temple of God, God will destroy him, because the temple of God is sacred; and you are that temple." [10]
The genuine Catholic does not pick and choose among the
teachings and directives of the magisterium as he would pick
and choose among the positions held in an political party, for
the latter are merely human, the former are divinely authenticated. He thinks with the Church.

The consecrated woman possesses a profound love for the
Church because this people is nothing less than a very communion of love. We have already dwelt on the frequency with
which Vatican II speaks of the Church as a communion or
assembly of love. [11] We may now conclude that the religious

congregation as a micro-ecclesia is a communion of love or it is nothing.[12] It goes without saying, then, that the individual member of this group loves the communion, all of it, not merely her special friends, or she is nothing. Yet one need not look long to find religious who see nothing incongruous in their cold manner toward those who disagree with them, in their tuning out whole groups in the Church, the Pope himself included. These persons may know the words about love, but one may question whether they know more than the surface of the reality. They can hardly know what the Church is all about, for she is an assembly of love. They can hardly know what God is all about, for he *is* love. They can hardly believe the divine judgment on the goodness of this people: "You grew more and more beautiful . . . The fame of your beauty spread through the nations, since it was perfect, because I had clothed you with my own splendor — it is the Lord Yahweh who speaks." [13]

The sister loves the Church as a mother because, under God, she has everything supernatural from her: Christ, Scripture, sacraments, counsels. Just as a natural mother need not be perfect to merit a singular love, so also members of the Church, even lofty members, need not be faultless to merit a special love. Filial gratitude plainly requires the religious to love this mother that has begotten her to life and still sustains her in it.

The sister loves the Church because the bleeding world needs a strongly united, loving Church. The problems we face are so complex, the evils so extensive and massive, that mere common sense dictates a deep union among those who are trying to solve those problems and dissolve those evils. How can mutually indifferent, and even more, openly hostile factions in a social body hope to meet successfully the vast and complex uncertainty, loneliness, injustice so rampant in the real world of this latter part of the twentieth century? Love must fill the Church if it is to fill the world. And if she is an ecclesial woman, love must fill the religious. Without it she is sounding brass and tinkling cymbal. All of which brings us to our next problem.

Criticism in the Church

Criticizing a beloved is admittedly a thorny problem. It is also an agony — if the person is really beloved. The fact of criticism in the Church is so plain and so widespread we need only notice it. Sensitivity to the problems this fact carries along with it is neither plain nor widespread. Only the naive or the reckless have simple views on the subject.

What can be so complex about criticizing churchmen? Even to ask this question betrays an innocence; yet we shall ask it and attempt some answers. If an ecclesial woman really loves the Church, all in it, not just her party, she has to come to a solution.

The first element in our problem is the gaping gulf that lies open between the biblical ideal of unity in the Church and the factual divisions that exist among us. The New Testament demands among Christians a unity not only of heart and will but also of mind and judgment. Paul would have the Philippians to be united in their convictions, to have a common mind.[14] Unless one drains these words of meaning, he can only see them as astonishing, as humanly impossible. There is to be no competition, no conceit; all are to be self-effacing.[15] To appreciate how astonishing this ideal is, one need only suppose that someone demand this intellectual unity of contemporary Catholics. Even more. Speaking of factions, party divisions in the Corinthian Church (does this sound familiar?), Paul appeals to his Christians to give up their differences and disagreements, to be united in belief and practice.[16] How many today pay any serious attention to this kind of admonition even in important matters? Yet Christ himself had prayed that our unity be so visible, tangible, striking that men may conclude from it that the incarnation had taken place.[17] Our unity is to be a motive of credibility, a miracle. Among early Christians oneness of mind and heart was obviously a miracle.[18] Is ours?

Gaping gulfs. What Henry Miller said of the human community in general we may say of segments in the Catholic community: "We are of one flesh but separated like stars." The divine promise assures us that basic Catholic unity will never fail, but it does not assure us that what we now see cannot happen. What do we now see? Gaping gulfs. We see not only polarizations of ultraconservatism and wild liberalism but also hostile polarizations. We see caricature in abundance — how, many describe the opposition with rigorous honesty? We see labeling, disposing of a statement by the easy expediency of putting it into a category — which obviously leaves untouched the question whether it is true or not. Positions are termed radical or conservative, forward-looking or traditional, personal or legal, and little attempt is made to shore up the emotion with evidence. We see tuning out on a vast scale: reading, listening to, talking with those who agree with us. One thinks it a mark of good sense to shun lectures or periodicals representing divergent viewpoints. We see evidences of the conceit St. Paul deplored — today it is expressed by considering the opposition as hopeless, a far cry from Paul's "always consider the other person to be better than yourself" (a remark made in a context dealing with intellectual disagreements).[19] We see men and women pronouncing on complex theological questions (e.g., action and contemplation) after having read one or two books or articles. Apparently they think this is doing one's homework. We see thousands rejecting a papal encyclical before having read it, rejecting a lecturer's statement before having wrestled with the evidence he has offered for it, jettisoning conciliar teaching even though it represents the work of 2000 bishops and 2000 theologians (not to mention the Holy Spirit). What can we name this, if arrogance is not the word? It is surely not the modesty of the scholar or the humility of the man of God or the openness of an ecclesial woman. When these people are religious, it is ironical that they consider themselves open, whereas they are in fact closed tight, the most closed in their congregation. They know the answers. Others are hopeless.

The second element in our problem of criticizing Church authorities is the problem of reserve and limit. We may note that history establishes both the need and the propriety of fraternal correction directed even to lofty members in the Church. Paul upbraiding Peter is only the first in a long series. Yet Scripture takes a dim view — to put it mildly — of those who murmur against Yahweh's representatives. To cite one example among many, we may recall that when Israel grumbled against Moses and Aaron, their grumbling was considered a rebellion against Yahweh, and when the community began to discuss stoning for their leaders, the Lord himself intervened: "How long will this people insult *me?*" [20] There is an identification of these men with God himself. This is why Christ will not tolerate rejection of his representatives; criticism, yes; rejection, no: "Anyone who listens to you listens to me; anyone who rejects you rejects me." [21] Trusting presentation of grievances, yes; disobedience, no. The reason: God himself stands behind every valid human authority: "All government comes from God . . . anyone who resists authority is rebelling against God's decision." [22]

There is yet another limit to criticism in the Church, a limit that is rarely noticed in the thinking of our day, a limit that runs exactly opposite to usual presuppositions. When the secular (or even religious) segment of a population rejects the preaching or practice of churchmen, it is tacitly supposed as obvious and needing no proof that most of the fault lies with the churchmen and/or their position. Ideals and principles are presumed without discussion to be wrong if large numbers of men feel them to be irrelevant or invalid. When I began to notice this presumption becoming a pattern it also began to strike me as a black/white view of reality: the world is always right, the Church is always wrong. Structure is benighted, subjects are enlightened. On purely logical grounds this approach struck me as naive, as arguing with the will rather than the intellect. And so I went further and decided to look into Scripture to discover how the New Testament viewed the rejection of the infant Church. I was embarrassed by what I found: it was more than I had bargained for. I was (and still am) unable to explain it fully. The New Testament's verdict seems to be a black and white squarely opposed to our contemporary black and white. Every time the gospels and epistles explain the rejection of the apostles or their message the whole blame is placed on the hearers of the word, not the preachers. Examples abound. We will cite only a few. In the parable of the sower the only reasons given for the fruitlessness of the divine preaching are the devil, rootlessness of the hearer, attachment to cares, riches, pleasures of life.[23] There is no hint that the message was badly presented. This is true not only of Christ but also of the apostles: "If anyone does not welcome you or listen to what you have to say, as you walk out of the house or town shake the dust from your feet. I tell you solemnly on the day of Judgment it will not go as hard with the land of Sodom and Gomorrah as with that town." [24] John's gospel has a whole series of texts that ascribe men's rejection of Jesus to the fact that "their deeds were evil." [25] St. Paul's judgment is the same.[26] Nowhere is there a hint that the human messengers are at fault. What to make of this? The reader may draw his own conclusions. We may cite a thought of Karl Rahner speaking of people who

> hold with a sort of mental obstinacy that more or less everything is wrong that the Church has in actual practice done in the course of history, except her solemn dogmatic definitions, — as though the life of the Church amounted to practically nothing but sin and falling away from the mind of Christ. Such people may imagine they have a heroic love for the Church of the "in spite of everything" sort. In fact, they consider themselves to possess a mind of superior discernment to that of the actual average everyday Church. They do not believe in the charismatic character that belongs to the Church's ministry even in the world of every day.[27]

We should like now to suppose that some policy, some structure, some authority in the Church is to be criticized. We suppose that the negative evaluation is needed, justified. We are asking at this point, how is it to be done? If Scripture sets down severe limits to the evaluation of sacred authorities and if rejection of those authorities is absolutely excluded by the will of Christ, how does one speak out?

The critic should begin by acknowledging himself to be ignorant and a sinner. He should admit at the outset to himself and to others that what the world needs most from him are not his words but his own continuing conversion. He should grant that others are his superiors, that he does not have all the answers. He should see that we already have too many little popes evaluating the real pope. The critic should begin with humility. He should start with truth.

Then he should notice the interesting fact that he is criticizing not an enemy, not a stranger, but a beloved. And this makes all the difference in the world. To grasp what the difference is one need only imagine the person on earth who is most dear to him and then visualize how he would go about the task of criticizing him. We can be sure, first of all, that he would have to be driven to criticize; he would not do it at the drop of a hat but only reluctantly. It should hurt him. The critic of the Church is evaluating a beloved, beloved for the reasons we have already considered. If he is not reluctant, if it does not pain him, he should stop in his tracks. He has a far more serious defect in himself. "Why do you observe the splinter in your brother's eye and never notice the plank in your own? How dare you say to your brother, 'Let me take the splinter out of your eye,' when all the time there is a plank in your own? Hypocrite! Take the plank out of your own eye first, and then you will see clearly enough to take the splinter out of your brother's eye." [28] Salutary advice. Not commonly heeded advice.

Secondly, our critic does his homework. He takes care to be enlightened, to see things straight, as they are. Otherwise we have caricature, perhaps calumny. When a man is driven to point out defects in a dearly beloved friend, he is sensitive to truth; he is sure of his facts. When a sister finds fault with her community, its policies or practices, she should know when to doubt her competency. Attendance at a few lectures, reading a book or several articles on religious obedience or poverty or silence does not bestow competency. It takes years of study, dozens of books (old and new), frequent discussion with many shades of opinion (not only with "my group") in order to acquire expertise in the problems of religious life. Yet there are not lacking hundreds of vocal critics who have not done their homework. And these are often the very ones who tune out those who have. Until one has done his homework he should be tentative in his judgments, slow to speak, eager to listen.

Criticism in the Church (or anywhere) should be both honest and unexaggerated: honest, because correction is an act of love; unexaggerated, because exaggeration is dishonest and it hurts the one we love. Rather than expand defects in his beloved, a man is at pains to find mitigating circumstances. He finds them honestly and they do not prevent him from speaking the truth. But he tries to see the whole truth.

He speaks to the right person. Paul spoke to Peter. He did not complain bitterly and to no advantage to a small coterie. He followed the Lord's manly admonition to go to the man himself, "If your brother does something wrong, go and have it out with him alone." [29] The ecclesial woman does not expose defects in the Church she loves any more than a lover would expose the faults of his beloved. She might do so if the matters were very serious and if she knew that in order to effect any change at all they would have to be exposed. However, because her concern springs from love, she not only studies the question first, but she checks her facts and avoids exaggerations as well. Her complaint is positively orientated toward achieving a good with the least harm. This is the way a lover corrects.

Finally, criticism in the Church is aimed at eventual har-

mony. We disagree in dialogue not to score points, not to win
a battle, but to find solutions, to achieve consensus. Christians
do not, or ought not to disagree as non-Christians may. A
people taught by the Holy Spirit ought to be able to achieve
a unity of mind because of the unity of the Source. Acrimonious
debate and, even worse, hostile tuning out of others — only
too present among both ultra-conservative and secularizing
religious women — bear none of the marks of the Holy Spirit:
warmth, humility, joy. "If love can persuade at all, or the
Spirit that we have in common, or any tenderness and sym-
pathy, then be united in your convictions." [30] Intellectual harmony is a feasible ideal because it was attained by mere men,
men who were docile to the Spirit: the early Christians were
of one heart and one soul.[31]

Love for the Church is a secure barometer of man's progress
toward God: "A man possesses the Holy Spirit to the measure
of his love for Christ's Church." [32] That Sister is advancing
in her spiritual life who is loyal to the Church even when she
speaks up, who listens to this Church and is willing to be
taught by her official teachers. She takes seriously those words,
"anyone who listens to you listens to me." [33] And she is very
much interested in listening to Christ.

Eucharistic Women

The Church's unity is caused by the
Eucharist. "The fact that there is only one loaf," says Paul,
"means that, though there are many of us, we form a single
body because we all have a share in this one loaf." [34] The
Mystical Body is given its unity by the physical Body. Why
is this so? The risen Lord whom we receive in this sacrament
is he who sends his Spirit of unity into our hearts. It is this
same Spirit who pours out love, the most unitive of all forces.
The Eucharist causes indwelling presence in the one Temple-
Church: "He who eats my flesh and drinks my blood lives
in me and I live in him." [35] Christ is the vine, we are the

branches. By dwelling in us with his Spirit he binds all his members into one. "Didn't you (plural) realize that you were God's temple (singular)?" [36]

Because she is an ecclesial woman, the sister is necessarily a eucharistic woman, which is to say also that she is a liturgical woman. Her daily participation in the Mass deepens her communion with her indwelling God.[37]

The Eucharistic orientation of consecrated virginity can be seen in many other ways. Because we have already dealt with some of these ideas in more general contexts we shall here content ourselves with noting relations to the Eucharist.

We may say in a basic sense that the Eucharist causes virginity. The virginal body of Christ born of the virginal body of Mary makes the consecration of virginity in the religious woman. The sister may say with St. Agnes, "When I love him I am chaste; when I touch him I remain pure; when I receive him, I am a virgin." [38] She may say this not only in the sense that "intimacy with him does not tarnish my purity" but much more that "intimacy with him *causes* my purity, my virginal consecration." Because consecrated virginity is more than a bodily condition, because it is a holy self gift to the Lord, it demands a sacred origin. The risen Christ is its source. A sister who easily gives up her vows (supposing she has a vocation to them) may well question the profundity of her eucharistic life.

Because this sacrament causes the divine indwelling, it also causes contemplation, the primary aim of consecrated virginity: undivided love, total concern for the things of the Lord, undistracted prayer.[39] Through this sacramental nourishment she grows in a profound communion with her Beloved: "He who eats my flesh and drinks my blood lives in me and I live in him." [40] There is a mutual, permanent in-living. This mutual in-living is a permanent communion effected by the transitory eating. The intersubjective communion of contemplation grows through this sacramental drinking. The thirst of the doe is slaked at the living stream.

The Eucharist and virginity imply a mutual giving of bodies. At the last supper the Lord had spoken those terrible, astonishing words, "This is my body which will be given for you," [41] a you that is not a nameless plurality but an individual, each and every individual: "The Son of God loved me and sacrificed himself for my sake." [42] The virgin likewise gives her body to the Lord and to him alone. In an entirely exalted manner Christ and his bride, the Church, mutually give and receive each other in the Mass. And who better images the virginal bridal character of the Church than the religious woman? She reflects plainly that the body "is for the Lord, and the Lord for the body . . . anyone who is joined to the Lord is one spirit with him." [43]

This mutual surrender of bodies includes a mutual sharing in the cross. The Eucharist looks back to Calvary; it renews the cross. "Until the Lord comes, therefore, everytime you eat this bread and drink this cup, you are proclaiming his death." [44] Renouncing as she does the great goods of marriage, self-disposition, property, the virgin lives the cross in her flesh. She receives much more in return,[45] yes, but her self gift is still a crucifixion. Sacrament and virgin are united on Calvary.

The religious woman learns to love in the sacrament of love. By love in this context we mean something unique, something found in the gospel and in those who live the gospel and nowhere else. Few of us fail to show warmth and cordiality to attractive persons close to us, but none of us finds it easy to show altruistic affection to everyone, absolutely everyone. Yet the universal love of Christ is our norm: "Just as I have loved you, you also must love one another." [46] This love is to be so extraordinary that it implies even a union of minds,[47] a oneness in convictions, a common mind,[48] one mind.[49] This is a miracle that can be born only from a miracle. This is a love union that can spring only from the body of the Lord. "As for loving our brothers, there is no need for anyone to write to you about that, since you have learnt from God yourselves to love one another." [50] The Christian virgin has chosen to live her charism in a community of ecclesially consecrated women of like mind. She must love her companions (and others) profoundly, warmly. She can learn virginal joy and affection only from the source of virginity and joy and love. The Eucharist transforms the woman into a virgin full of love.

For all these reasons the sister is a eucharistic woman. She is deeply attuned both to the liturgical reenactment of Calvary and to the abiding presence of her Lord on the altar. She has studied the theology that explains the inner relations between Mass, thanksgiving, visits to the Blessed Sacrament, and she lives those relationships. She "prizes daily conversation with Christ the Lord in visits of personal devotion to the most Holy Eucharist." [51] She joins herself to the people of God who "gather and find help and comfort through venerating the presence of the Son of God our Savior, offered for us on the sacrificial altar." [52] She is a model to all men who are to be hidden with Christ in God.[53] She illumines for this people those absolute words of the psalmist: "I look to no one else in heaven, I delight in nothing else on earth. My flesh and my heart are pining with love, my heart's Rock, my own, God forever! ... My joy lies in being close to God." [54] Closeness to the Eucharistic God brings closeness to men.

Virgin, a Maximalist

Because virginity is a charism of total self-reservation, total self-gift to the Lord, because the virgin is a woman whose undivided heart is centered on him and his affairs, she is necessarily a maximalist. Every man, of course, before the Lord God must be a maximalist. Scripture is forever repeating that we must seek our God with a whole heart, that we love with all our strength, that we vehemently long for him, that we be perfect even as he is perfect, that we run, not walk toward him. Anyone who knows Scripture knows this unflinching, unconditional, unlimited call. And anyone who has experienced the inner grace of the Holy Spirit knows that his grace not only calls, it impels. The further one goes and grows, the more he knows that anything less than everything is not enough.

The ecclesial woman should know this best of all. She is pure and poor and obedient precisely that she may more easily be freed for totality. Love is the *raison d'etre* of her surrender and love knows no limit. She stands before the people of God as a symbol of the complete God-centeredness demanded of every man. She witnesses to the overriding necessities of the kingdom that brook no dilution, no diminishment, no compromise. One does not whittle a bargain with God. She stands as a sign in the flesh that the Lord is really the Lord. He is not merely one next to others. Not merely the first. Not merely the greatest. He is the absolute fullness, purest beauty, brightest awareness, deepest love. She stands in the flesh a witness to undiminished response to unlimited call:

"I look to no one else in heaven, I
delight in nothing else on earth." [55]

"None of you can be my disciples unless
he gives up all his possessions." [56]

"The effects of light are seen in
complete goodness." [57]

"You must therefore be perfect just as
your heavenly Father is perfect." [58]

"You must love the Lord your God with
all your heart, with all your soul,
with all your strength, and with all
your mind." [59]

The virgin reminds men that they are not legalists, men interested in fulfilling only the letter of the law, men so dry

that they cannot think beyond an obligation horizon. The consecrated woman stands for a love morality, and openarmedness
that freely gives everything to the Beloved. She is a sign of
deep prayer and total commitment to the apostolate. The virgin
is a maximalist. She is the glory of her people.

Maternal Love in the Church

Though the Church is often accused
of being male-dominated, she is more feminine than she is
masculine. We speak of the Church as "she," Mother — we
naturally shrink from "he" or Father in reference to her. This
feeling of the faithful is theologically sound. The Church is
feminine in relation to Christ: she is virgin, bride, mother.
And so is the consecrated woman virgin, bride, mother. In
realizing her womanliness the sister is teaching the Church how
to be the Church: loyal, faithful, receptive, totally given to
Christ in contemplation and service. The sister teaches a
maternal care, how to love warmly and generously. Perhaps
this is why Vatican II admonished all in the Church engaged
in the apostolate, men as well as women, to find in Mary
"an example of maternal love by which *all* should be fittingly
animated." [60]

We have here a basic reason why religious women should be
brought to cooperate more intimately into the workings of the
parish, diocese, and Roman congregations. This is so not only
because the feminine sex deserves greater recognition in the
Church but also because the Church needs the feminine sex
more than has been realized.

Religious Profession not a Sacrament

We have developed in our first chapter
the proposition that the religious woman is sacramental. If this
is so, one would expect that the act by which she becomes

a religious would be numbered among the seven symbol-bearers of grace. Yet it is not. Even more: the seven sacraments are meant to heal and help, to rouse and redeem, to give life and strength. Does not the virgin, as well as the wife, need in her way of life healing and helping, rousing and redeeming, life and strength? Still more: if consecrated virginity is objectively superior to marriage, as twenty centuries of Catholic tradition up to and including Vatican II affirm, why is it not initiated by a sacrament in a sacramental economy? Good questions. We may suggest several answers.

First of all, virginity is a baptismal life, baptism lived without reservation. It is deeply rooted in baptismal consecration, observes Vatican II, and more fully manifests it.[61] Virginity is already sacramental, and so at religious profession a young girl re-affirms her baptism as an ecclesial woman. She commits herself to live everything in the gospel, counsel as well as commandment. Her profession is a proclamation of baptism lived to the hilt.

Secondly, earthly marriage is a *sign* of the pilgrim marriage of Christ and his Church, whereas virginity is the real thing itself, not only a sign of the real thing.

Thirdly, virginity pertains especially to the marriage of Christ and the Church in the eschaton, a "time" of no sacraments, a "time" when a sacramental economy shall give way to facial vision and direct contact. This is why there is no incongruity in marriage being a sacrament and religious profession not being one. Our future non-sacramental state shall be superior to our present sacramental lot.

Scriptural Women

An ecclesial woman is necessarily a biblical woman, for the recorded word of God belongs to the integral reality that is the Church. Contemporary theological insight stresses the unity of sacred tradition and Sacred Scripture in one deposit of God's word. Writers speak of the Church, tradition and Scripture as one whole with each element including the others. As an ecclesial person, therefore, the religious immerses herself in the holy word of God and in the living tradition that surrounds and interprets it.

There are specific reasons, too, why the virgin is biblical. She has built her whole life on faith. It is a drastic kind of life that is hardly intelligible except on the premise of faith. After the pattern of the first consecrated Virgin the religious is blessed because she has believed. She has taken God at his word and has staked her whole destiny on it. She really operates on the promise that those who give up everything, house and home, husband and children, for the gospel receive immeasurably more in return even in this present time.

The virgin is biblical because she is contemplative. The primary purpose of her consecration is profound communion with her indwelling Beloved. Scripture becomes part of her dialogue: "Prayer should accompany the reading of Sacred Scripture, so that God and man talk together; for 'we speak to Him when we pray; we hear Him when we read the divine sayings.' " [62] Both testaments are likened to a mirror in which the Church of earth looks at God.[63] The religious imitates Mary seated at the feet of Christ absorbed in his word. She drinks from the divine spring the words that are "new life for the soul . . . wisdom for the simple . . . joy for the heart . . . light for the eyes." [64] Her virginal freedom opens her to truth lived in joyful love.

The virgin is biblical because she is mother through the word. Like Paul she can say to her children "I must go through the pain of giving birth to you all over again, until Christ is formed in you," for it is through the Good News that she begets them.[65] She knows that the word that proceeds from the mouth of Yahweh does not return to him empty but carries out his will and does what it was sent to do.[66] She is a woman of this word and she is mother by it . . . just as the Church herself is mother by it.

Ecclesiality of Contemplation

"It is of the *essence* of the Church that she be both . . . eager to act and yet devoted to contemplation." [67]

The ecclesial woman is essentially contemplative. She is also essentially eager to act, of course. We have already said this at length in our second chapter. Many others have likewise said it. We all know it. But all of us do not know the cruciality of contemplation. Some of us may even question Vatican II's statement that contemplation is essential to the Church.

Unless one is willing to embrace an ecclesiastical extrinsicism, a moment's reflection will assure him that contemplation must indeed be essential to the people of God. What is this contemplation if not a profound intersubjective communion with the Lord abiding within? And who can advance a single sound theological argument to support the contention that communing with men is more important than communing with God? Who could successfully fend off the reproach of pharisaism from those who worship with word and ceremony but with scant love from the heart? If the Church were not contemplative, she would be subject to that ancient condemnation: you worship me with your lips but your heart is far from me. If the Church were not contemplative, she would be unfaithful to her Head who, says Luke, "would always go off to some place where he could be alone and pray." Yes, if a man, any man, takes the putting on of the total Christ seriously, if he avoids a selective reading of the gospels, he will be contemplative.

Such is simple theological fact. How does this fact fit into the life of the religious woman? We have elsewhere discussed her prayer life as ecclesially orientated. We need now only to underline the realization that the sister in solitude at prayer is ecclesial because she is at the heart of the Church. She is reliving the communing of Jesus with his Father in their Spirit. The virgin in the Church is concerned with the Lord's affairs, how she may pray without distraction. Even if she belongs to an apostolic congregation, her vocation is first of all a vocation to prayer.[68] She is the Church's public prayer person in her "devotion to contemplation." She is to be a model of the Church experiencing her Lord, tasting to their full of the paschal mysteries, grasping the creed in deed, being set on fire by the Eucharist.[69] She is a reminder to all the people of God that in their private homes they are to enter their own rooms and pray to the Father without ceasing.[70] She is to teach the Church how to join community living to prayerful solitude, how to fill man's gaping emptiness with the joyful peace that surpasses understanding.[71] What Vatican II said of the Church at large we must say of the virgin: It is of the essence of the consecrated woman that she be both eager to act and yet devoted to contemplation. Why? She is an ecclesial woman.

Virgin: Ecclesial Sacrifice

The Church must walk the same road which Christ walked . . . self-sacrifice to the death.[72]

The Lord has given his body for his Church: "This is my body which will be given for you." [73] The virgin gives her body to the Lord and to him only.[74] The virginal mystery is an ecclesial mystery and a marriage mystery. It is, therefore, a mutual gift mystery, a mutual sacrifice destined to life.

We must, then, raise the question of mortification and penance in the ecclesial-religious context. This context is, first of all, that of the whole people of God, a people who are living a moral revolution, not simply a refinement of Aristotelian or Platonic ethics: "Your mind must be renewed by a spiritual revolution." [75] And the purpose of the moral upheaval is the creation of a "new self . . . created in God's way." [76] An essentialist ethic is based on an abstract man, the man of pure nature, a man who does not exist. An ethic of mere reason, of mere common sense deals with a figment of conceptual thought, good as far as it goes, but not going far enough. An existential ethic accepts the essentialist truth but sees it in real man, man who is infected with the deleterious effects of original sin. Mortification, therefore, may not be judged by common sense alone but by the gospel first of all. The evangelical revolution will not contradict common sense, but it will puzzle it, transcend it, transform it.

Now the revolutionary plan for creating a new self demands a dying of the old self. No half measure suffices. The New Testament is uncompromising even though popularizers of it may be; "Anyone who wants to save his life will lose it." [77] Period. "Unless a wheat grain falls on the ground and dies, it remains only a single grain; but if it dies, it yields a rich harvest." [78] Unvarnished condition. "If in union with Christ we have imitated his death, we shall also imitate him in his resurrection. We must realize that our former selves have been crucified with him . . . ." [79] And so one could go on, citing text after text demanding self-denial, complete detachment, carrying of the cross, chastisement of the body. Vatican II is simply being faithful to the gospel when it proclaims that "the church must walk the same road which Christ walked . . . self-sacrifice to the death."

This, too, is the road the virgin must walk if she is to be faithful to her ecclesial vocation. She who has given her body to the Lord should stand as a beacon in the midst of the Mystical Body, as symbol to a people who die to live. She declares in her person that Christian self-denial is a participation in Christian death, for she gives up in the bloom of her youth what every man must surrender at his last breath: property, marriage, free self-disposition. The layman should be reminded by the religious that his involvement in the temporal order is transitory, is pointed eventually to the eternal order. He should recall from her austerity that the gospel is preached to everyone; self-denial, poverty, detachment, crucifixion. He learns from her life that resurrection follows only after a previous death.

Because all men, worldly and unworldly alike, expect a

professed religious to be all this, they easily pity or despise her when she is not. The shortest path religious may take to a debilitating ineffectiveness, even to being despised, is to indulge in gay-blade living. The path is short because it is psuedo. To want the joys of two worlds and the sacrifices of neither is to want a living lie. A crossless Christianity is no Christianity. An unascetical religious is living a facade. She is neither symbol nor substance, neither evangelical nor ecclesial.

Virgin and Secularity

Whatever position one may take regarding the degree of secularization a given nation of the world may or may not have reached, one thing is beyond doubt: the Christ of the gospels was thoroughly an unsecular figure. He did not show the least interest in the purely secular. The whole atmosphere in which he thought and moved was the sacred: his Father's will, repentance by men, a holy love for neighbor, whole nights in prayer. We are by no means denying that he wanted the temporal order cared for in loyalty, justice and love, but simple honesty requires us to note that he devoted mighty little attention to it. And when he did turn his mind to the subject he repeatedly emphasized the secondary character of the secular. Three examples among many will illustrate our point. "Do not say, 'What are we to eat? What are we to drink? How are we to be clothed? [80] It is the pagans who set their hearts on all these things. Your heavenly Father knows you need them all. Set your hearts on his kingdom *first* . . . As for the part that fell into thorns, this is people who have heard, but as they go on their way they are choked by the worries and riches and pleasures of life and do not reach maturity . . .[81] None of you can be my disciple unless he gives up all his possessions." [82] By any standard these are stark statements. And there are dozens of others like them in the gospels and in the Acts, Paul, James. Vatican II speaks in the same vein. While the council repeatedly refers to the lay-man's task in the secular city, it infuses into its discussion a sacred orientation and permeation. It teaches the same other-worldliness and detachment and poverty the gospels teach.

If this is true of all the people of God, we may ask how the religious fits into the picture. Is she secular in any sense? How does she differ from a layman on this score. One can get the feel for this problem by contrasting the notably different ways in which Vatican II consistently refers to the one state and the other. We may suggest some of these differences. Ac-cording to the council the

religious	*layman*
a.) gives testimony to the bea-titudes and lives the coun-sels (CC #31, 43, 44, 46)	a.) possesses a secular quality that is *proper* to him (CC #31)
b.) shows that God's kingdom is superior to all earthly considerations (CC #44)	b.) sanctifies the temporal or-der after the manner of leaven (CC #31; DMAC #15)
c.) is totally dedicated to God (CC #44)	c.) permeates the world with the spirit of Christ (CC #36; DLA #2, 4; DMSC #3)
d.) renounces the world . . . lives a life hidden with Christ (DRL #5, 6)	d.) spends his days in the midst of the world (DLA #2; DMAC #15)
e.) engages in God's service (DRL #5)	e.) engages in secular duties

This consistent pattern makes clear that while the layman is a secular person, the religious is not. Obviously this does not mean that the laymen lacks sacredness or that the religious has no involvement in the secular. But it does clearly mean that the religious is not within the secular as the layman is.

We may not fail to notice that Vatican II attributes to the lay person a secular quality that is *proper* to him.[83] The word, proper, in a theological context means belonging to a thing in an exclusive way. Discursive reasoning is proper to man — no other being thinks in this way. What, then, is this secular quality that is proper to the layman and not shared by the religious?

Once we have granted that every man's destiny is the facial vision and delight in triune Beauty we have granted that man's center of gravity has been shifted out of this world into the enthralling mystery of God. There shall indeed be a new heaven and a new earth enjoyed in a risen body, but terrestrial splendor shall be peripheral to the core issue, the transfiguring embrace with pure Love and Joy. In saying this we are saying that every man is unsecular in basic thrust and destiny. Yet every man wins his destiny on the stage of this world and no other. Differences between laymen and religious are differences of manner in winning this destiny. The layman's daily concern is the temporal order: marriage, business, politics. He lives and works in this order as yeast in a loaf. He mingles and penetrates. The bulk of his time is spent in the midst of the world and in its concerns. The religious on the other hand is committed totally to divine service: contemplation, worship, ecclesial apostolate, evangelical-virginal community. The sister is a woman of divine transcendence and immanence, a sacred symbol, a sacrament of salvation, an ecclesial person. She is sacred, not secular.

These observations do not settle the question as to what, if any, substantial difference there may or may not be between religious and secular institutes.[84] We are not suggesting that the members of the latter are secular in the same senses that (other) laymen are — there are obviously points of contact and points of divergence. As soon as one seriously embraces the evangelical counsels he has left the world in a radical way that the ordinary layman has not left it. He has left everything the usual man yearns for: a wife (husband), family, property, self-disposition. He retains a close contact with his fellowmen, but he has all the same radically parted company from them. Even his entrance into the secular world is not secular, but sacred.

The same conclusion emerges as soon as one reflects on what is meant by calling a sister an *ecclesial* woman. Every page of this book shows that she is sacred, not secular. In point of fact, when St. Paul draws the distinction between the married and the virgin it is precisely on the basis of the latter being directly concerned with the Lord. And that is the difference between the secular and the sacred. Attempts, therefore, to secularize the religious life are self-contradictory. They are saved from being ludicrous only by the theological innocence of their authors. Untenable, too, are the efforts to rub out the distinction between layman and religious. Neither Scripture nor the magisterium nor Catholic tradition supports an identification of these states in life. There is, of course, no doubt that all men pursue essentially the same sanctity — Christification is one for all.

The practical consequences of what we are saying are considerable. If the first norm of renewal is the gospel, updating can never mean secularization. Religious may (and must) be aided by new findings in psychology and sociology, but these areas of knowledge cannot supply the basic guiding norms for ecclesial renewal. Only Christ can. Secondly, the religious woman finds her basic fulfillment in God, not in man. This is true of any woman, of course: "Those *who seek Yahweh* lack nothing good." [85] God is the center of the universe, not man. Christianity is not a refined humanism. Of all women the virgin should know that communion with men, good and necessary as it is, is not enough. Only the divine enough is really enough: "Rest in God *alone,* my soul!" [86] Thirdly, religious live not as members of a women's club but as virgins in ecclesial community, which is to say, as sacred women in sacred community. They pray and work together, they go out warmly to all other men together. They are a sacred team

united by and in and for the Eucharist. Fourthly, consecrated
women live the cross because they accept the whole gospel.
The crucified one is a scandal and madness to the worldling
and nonsense to the sensual man,[87] but to the virgin who has
the Spirit the cross is the wisdom and power of God. She
knows that her Master had to suffer those things to enter into
his glory,[88] and she knows she is no greater than he. She is
eager to take up her cross daily and deny herself actively . . .
because he did. She has put on the mind of Christ, not the
merely secular mind, and she is obedient even to death on
a cross.[89] She takes seriously the admonition of Paul: "Let
your thoughts be on heavenly things, not on the things that
are on earth, because you have died." [90] Lastly, the ecclesial
woman does not dilute the gospel on the plea of being relevant. She is not ashamed of the gospel. Relevance, by all
means. She asserts that the only basic relevance to a bleeding,
despairing world is the crucified, risen Jesus. Without this key
the puzzle is forever locked. Secularization only prolongs the
agony.

Finality of Virginity

Why religious women? Is there one
reason for this vocation or several? If several, what is their
relative significance? Are these reasons what we have traditional-
ly thought them to be or do we now possess radically new
insights into them? Is the virginal vocation primarily individual
or social? Does it aim first at personal fulfillment and secondly
at the people of God at large?

The finality of a call must begin with the caller. For what
reason(s) does God plant the virginal vocation in a girl's
heart? We can perhaps best understand her call in the light
of Yahweh's many calls to his representatives in the course of
salvation history.

We notice first of all that Yahweh calls individuals *for the people,* the one for the many.[91] Abraham is summoned from his home and his country because the Lord will make him "father of a *multitude* of nations." Yet Abraham is called for his own sake too.

> I will establish my Covenant between myself and *you,* and your *descendants* after you, generation after generation, a Covenant in perpetuity, to be *your* God and the God of your *descendants* after you. I will give to *you* and to your *descendants* after you the land you are living in.[92]

Joseph is called for the group: "God sent me before you to preserve *your lives* . . . God sent me before you to make sure that your *race* would have survivors . . . ." [93] Moses is called to save himself and the sons of Israel: "I send you to Pharaoh to bring the *sons* of Israel, my people, out of Egypt." [94] Gideon is summoned to save the nation: "Yahweh is with you, valiant warrior . . . Go in the strength now upholding you, and you will rescue Israel from the power of Midian." [95] The great Isaiah hears the mission: "Go, and say to this *people.*" [96] Jeremiah is sent "as prophet to the *nations* . . . to *those* to whom I send you . . . over *nations* and over kingdoms." [97]

The new dispensation is no different. John the Baptist is sent from his mother's womb to bring back *"many* of the sons of Israel to the Lord their God . . . to give *his people* knowledge of salvation." [98] Mary brings forth "the salvation . . . prepared for *all the nations to see."* [99] And this incarnated Salvation calls apostles to be fishers of *men,* to go into the *whole world* and preach the gospel to every creature.[100] Some men are to embrace celibacy for the sake of the kingdom. Though the New Testament presents the apostolic vocation as a call for the group, it envisions the counsels of virginity and poverty as deeply beneficial to the individual's personal growth. One who gives up property and marriage receives a hundredfold in this life itself, a far more fulfilling personal return. The virgin is a virgin that her heart may be undivided, that she may pray without distraction, that she may be concerned with the affairs of the Lord. Since the Lord's affairs are centered in the *ecclesia,* the virgin is, of course, concerned with all of God's people. From the biblical point of view, therefore, a man or woman is called by the Lord both for the group and for personal fulfillment. Vocation is at once social and individual. According to difference in emphasis the apostolic vocation seems to stress the group first and the individual second, whereas the virginal-poor call envisions the individual first and the group second. How may we specify this dual finality as it applies to the religious woman? Why does a girl consecrate herself a virgin to the Lord?

Proximately and practically she is responding to a particular call of love addressed to her as a unique person of inestimable value. This call is also a particular charism bestowed on her for the good of all men. She is not therefore simply applying a universal abstract principle to her own situation. She is a person responding to a Person. She who has received a gift is giving herself as a total gift. For a virgin is a total self gift.

We may be more specific still. Why does the virgin reserve herself for the Lord alone? [101] She wants freedom, utter freedom for an exclusive, untrammeled love for her God and a universal love for men. The virgin wants everything. The world is not large enough for her. That is why she needs a large heart. She wants utter freedom for contemplation, for drinking Reality and reality.

She wants freedom also for *complete* availability to the Church and her apostolic mission. This availability concerns not only time but also scope. Surely, the entire hour-by-hour life of the consecrated woman is given to the Lord and his own. But her availability to the Church includes her heart. Her complete attention, concern, love are directed to the things of the Lord. A girl becomes a religious because she wants an entirety of availability to her God in his Church. We have noted from many points of view how this is so, how she is so thoroughly an ecclesial woman.

The virgin is a beacon. She has come also to witness. Some men do not like what she stands for, but she remains a beacon. She is so different from the usual run of women that one cannot be indifferent to her. In this she is again like Christ. Before him no man can be neutral. He who is not for him is against him. So with the virgin of Christ. Everything about her is eloquent about him. Her pure self-reservation is a reservation for him. She is poor to proclaim his poverty that the world may be rich. She is obedient for him who was obedient to death. In her being she proclaims that the goods of earth, good though they be, are not ultimate, that men are to seek first the kingdom of God and holiness — and all the rest will be added.

Finally, a girl becomes a religious because she wishes to do all these things, to live these various finalities in an intensely Christian community. She wishes to join a virginal community and live her particular charism in a group possessing a general charism. She wishes to attain the enlightenment, support, affection, inspiration she needs from other consecrated women of like mind. She wants to live virginal love, availability, service, witness in union with other ecclesial women who have found that Christ is the only answer to the human puzzle. She is a total self-gift in a sacred ecclesial community.

These are the reasons a woman becomes a religious.

Pre-eminence of Virginity

An omnipresent but unexpressed implication in what we have been saying has probably more than once intruded itself into the reader's mind. The writer confesses that he has not consciously pressed this implication, nor has he always even been aware of it. A moment's reflection, however, makes it plain: if the religious woman is ecclesial in all the manifold ways we have considered, her way of life enjoys a singular eminence. We might as well be honest and say that eminence here means superiority. And this currently is an unpopular thing to say in some circles. Rather than enter into a polemic we shall note briefly why this position is rejected by some and accepted by others. We wish to spend most of our time viewing the question from the standpoint of this whole book.

The first view. Virginity and marriage should not be compared because they are complementary states in the Christian dispensation. They are different but equal, not to be ranked. Furthermore, states in life are subjective, not merely objective matters. That state is best which is subjectively best for a person. One should not speak of marriage and virginity as though they were given "out there," aside from persons, but only as they are proposed to Paul or Susan. If Paul is called to marriage, that is best for him, whereas if Susan is called to the religious life, that is best for her. Lastly, the very idea of ranking states of life strikes many people as a slur on the lesser state. It seems undemocratic, unfair, perhaps even conceited. A man ought to be judged according to his personal merit, not according to his station in life.

The second position can be summarized in four statements: 1.) There *is* an objective question of value in states of life. 2.) They are to be compared. 3.) Virginity is objectively superior to marriage. 4.) There is here no belittling of marriage or comparison of subjective holiness. This position has been the constant teaching of the magisterium beginning with the gospels and St. Paul [102] on through the patristic literature and the Council of Trent and culminating in Vatican II and the recent encyclical of Pope Paul VI on celibacy.[103] We do not envision our present task to include a thoroughgoing exposition of the Church's mind, but we may note that we have not seen a single current effort to set this doctrine aside that has been able to avoid tortuous treatment of texts as a means of evading the clear content of scriptural, conciliar and papal pronouncements. We do see our task, however, as including a few brief comments on the first view and a summarizing exposition of how a Catholic theology of the sister as an ecclesial woman demands the second position.

The arguments for the first position are defective. One can easily grant that virginity and marriage are complementary ways of life, (this is an obvious truth) without any need to hold a consequent equality. Spirit and matter in man are complementary but of unequal ontological rank. The sexes are complementary (and equal in personal worth and dignity) but unequal in many ways. Bees and flowers are complementary but unequal. One could go on and on. This argument proves nothing. Secondly, to say that states in life are to be judged on the basis of subjective suitability to an existing person is to utter a truth, but only a partial truth. States in life are objective realities even though they actually exist only in persons. One may discuss the relative rank of sensitivity and spirituality even though they exist only in concrete animals and spirits. We may say that marriage is best for Susan but we leave untouched the valid question about the objective value of marriage aside from Susan. Virginity and marriage are specifiable ways of achieving fulfillment and as ways or means they can be compared. Flying by plane, driving a car, walking on foot are ways of getting from Chicago to New York. The goal is the same in each case, but the efficiency of the means varies. The goal of perfect holiness is identical for all men, but the means vary in effectiveness. And means are objective matters. They can, and sometimes ought to be compared. Finally, to assert the superiority of virginity is not to belittle marriage. Some persons see only good and bad and scarcely appreciate good and better. And it should be clear to anyone that there is no comparison of persons. The universal call to holiness is universal.

Summarizing three chapters in two pages is no easy task

and yet we must now attempt to do it. From the point of view
of evangelical totality and ecclesiality we shall show some of
the differences between virginity and marriage by juxtaposing
and thus comparing the two states in life.

Virginity	*Marriage*
1. Direct, non-sacramental relationship to God, characteristic of eternal life	1. Sacramental state of this present time destined to cede to a non-sacramental state
2. More deeply rooted in baptismal consecration and *more* intimately joined to the mystery of the Church	2. Lacks this *special* (more-ness) rooting and this *special* joining
3. Proper sphere is the sacred	3. Proper sphere is the secular
4. *Immediately* orientated to the transforming union, a spiritual marriage between God and woman	4. *Immediately* orientated to an earthly marital union between man and woman
5. Lives total gospel, counsels and precepts, to their full	5. Lives the gospel but not the counsels to their full
6. Attempts to imitate Christ and Mary in all	6. Does not attempt this total imitation — cf. #7
7. Freedom achieved through virginity and vowed poverty	7. These means to freedom unavailable
8. More easily lives the total renunciations of the gospel: "None of you can be my disciple unless he gives up all	8. Radical detachment is more difficult to achieve though it applies to the married also

his possessions." Lk
14:33

9. Tailor-made to relive
Christ's prayer life: "He
would *always* go off
to some place where he
could be alone and
pray." Lk 5:16

9. Many impediments to
this kind of prayer
life — yet continual
prayer in the gospel is
directed to all men
as an ideal

10. Hundredfold is promised
to those who give up
wife, lands . . .

10. This not promised to
the married

11. Possession of an
undivided heart: 1 Cor
7

11. Heart is divided, "torn
two ways"

12. Spared "tribulations of
the flesh": 1 Cor 7

12. Subject to these
troubles

13. Reflects the virginity of
the Church

13. Does not reflect this
characteristic

14. Concern with "things of
the Lord" renders
contemplation easier in
itself

14. Concern with secular
affairs renders
contemplation more
difficult

15. Totally available to
apostolate of the
Church and universal
love

15. Availability for
apostolate severely
limited during most
years of married life

16. A new sign of God's
victorious grace, achieved
sanctity

16. A sign of victorious
grace and achieved
sanctity but not so
obviously visible and
communal

17. Immediately orientated
to. supernatural
motherhood

17. Immediately orientated
to natural motherhood

18. Witness to man's final
consummation

18. Witness to temporal
affairs of this age

19. Virginal life continues on uninterruptedly into eternal life	19. Married life ceases at death

Indeed, the Catholic theoolgian must confess "the superiority of virginity consecrated to Christ." [104] The complete chastity that religious profess

> deserves to be esteemed as a *surpassing* gift of grace. For it liberates the human heart in a *unique way* and causes it to burn with *greater love* for God and all mankind. It is therefore an *outstanding token* of heavenly riches, and also *a most suitable* way for religious to spend themselves readily in God's service and in works of the apostolate. Religious thereby give witness to all Christ's faithful of that wondrous marriage between the Church and Christ her only spouse, a union which has been established by God and will be fully manifested in the world to come.[105]

The religious woman lives a surpassing charism, a unique way to a greater love. She is an ecclesial woman who lives the life of the Church on earth in prayer and service, a life that is a wondrous marriage with the Word Incarnate, a marriage begun now but fully manifested only when eye sees what cannot now be seen, when ear hears what is now beyond hearing, when the unimaginable God shows himself as he unspeakably is.

Epilogue: *A Word on Relevance*

In a society which sees one institution after another slowly disintegrate and finally disappear one might expect doubts to arise regarding the stability even of centuries-old religious congregations. These casual doubts may grow into strong persuasions when one observes contemporary phenomena in religious life: sharp drops in interested candidates, large numbers of veteran members leaving, polarities among some of those who remain, identity confusions among many of the others. It was almost inevitable that serious people would question the durability of the religious life and its relévance in the world we know. Nor is this questioning new. One need only recall the vigorous responses of Thomas and Bonaventure to the harsh attacks of their day upon the evangelical counsels as a way of human existence.

Even granted all that we have said in this volume, we would offer no comforting assurance that each and every religious congregation shall survive our age of transition: some are disintegrating and disappearing before our very eyes. We see little future to unbending conservatism on the one hand and a naive secularization on the other. Relevance demands change because man is incarnated in a changing world, and yet it also demands authentic identity because sham constructions are soon stripped and shown for what they are.

Norms for judging the relevance of the Christic new creation are by no means obvious to all men. In point of fact as the gospels present these norms they flatly contradict most of our usual expectations. The average man, religious or otherwise, judges relevance by poll results, public acclaim, general acceptability. By these standards the asceticism of the gospel could not be more irrelevant. When the Pharisees were presented with Jesus' uncompromising detachment doctrine, they "heard all this and laughed at him." Then came the divine judgment on human norms of relevance: "What is thought highly of by men is loathsome in the sight of God." [1] Paul averts that to the sensual man spiritual things are nonsense.[2] Since God's thoughts are incomparably elevated beyond man's gropings, religious life cannot be judged by mere popular standards. It is to be judged by the gospel or it is not to be judged.[3]

When, therefore, we ask about the relevance of the religious life, we are not asking about its general acceptability or popularity. Of course, it is not popular. The whole of the gospel (e.g., hell and penance as well as resurrection and joy) is not popular and never has been popular. We are asking rather whether the life of the counsels responds to the deepest needs of real men in a real world. Those congregations that do respond to real needs with a genuinely Christian existence have every reason to be optimistic about their future. Because the divine word can never pass away, a life style immersed in the word and faithful to it will never pass away. Because it is thoroughly biblical and ecclesial, the religious life as such can never totally disappear. We would consequently answer our relevance question in these ways:

If God is both transcendent and immanent, we shall always need men and women heroic enough to renounce all things (Lk 14:33), to stake everything in a witness to Him as incomparably Other and yet as incomparably close.

If God is God (and not a god whittled down to human proportions), there must always be men who *obviously* live for Him alone.

If man as incarnated spirit is dynamically orientated to the absolute Mystery, we need men to show clearly what being fully human means.

If the celibate existence of Christ Jesus has perduring meaning, the virgin is forever meaningful.

If the voluntary factual poverty of the incarnate Word is to be lived in the world and for the reasons for which He lived it, the counsel of poverty remains relevant even in an affluent society.

If the Church herself is a pilgrim poor community of love, some among her must continue to sell all they have, share in common, live in love . . . even without blood relationship.

If the apostolic activity animated by the Spirit is team and ecclesial, a religious apostolate could not be more significant.

If the Church is a virgin mother, we need individual virgin mothers to enflesh her reality in a visible manner.

If Christ Jesus "would always go off to some place where he could be alone and pray," (Lk 5:16) the world must always

find men and women devoted to contemplation as reminders
that all men are made to drink Beauty in prayer.

If by evangelical renunciation a disciple receives a greater
fulfillment, is "repaid a hundred times over" in the world (Mt
19:29), a more relevant life cannot be found.

In other words, if man is really an incarnated thirst for the
infinite and if he really believes the whole gospel, he has already granted the relevance of the religious life. The life of
the evangelical counsels is permanent because Christ Jesus is
permanent. "Jesus Christ is the same today as he was yesterday
and as he will be forever." [4]

NOTES FOR CHAPTER ONE

1. Perhaps these frequent expressions, "particular way, special manner," should be considered plain invitations to creative theological speculations explaining what particular and special may mean.
2. John L. McKenzie, *Dictionary of the Bible*, p. 133.
3. CL #2.
4. Ps 143:6.
5. Ps 145: 8, 9, 17, 3.
6. Ps 145:3.
7. 1 Tim 6:16.
8. Jn 1:14.
9. 1 Jn 1:1-2.
10. CL #2.
11. "The religious state reveals in a unique way that the kingdom of God and its overmastering necessities are superior to all earthly considerations." CC #44.
12. DPOB #33.
13. DRL #5.
14. Ps 139; Acts 17:28.
15. Jn 14:15-23.
16. 1 Jn 4:16.
17. Hab 2:20.
18. Ps 42-3:1-2.
19 Lk 5:16.
20. Jn 14:10-11.
21. Lk 22:36.
22. 1 Cor 13:12..
23. Jn 17:3.
24. 1 Cor 2:9.
25. CC #6.
26. 1 Cor 3:16-17; 6:19-20.
27. 1 Pet 2:5.
28. For a more complete discussion of this truth see our article "Virginal Temple," *Review for Religious*, January, 1968, 27:21-43.
29. DRL #5. Cf. 1 Cor 7:32-34.
30. Ps 62:1, 5.
31. Ps 119:10.
32. Pss 42-43:1-2; 63:1; 84:2.

33. Pss 42-43:8; 63:6; 77:2, 6; 84:4; Lk 22:36; 1 Thess 5:17, etc.

34. 1 Cor 7:35.

35. CL #2.

36. *Ibid.*

37. DPOB #33.

38. DMAC #18.

39. Ps 73:25-26, 28.

40. Rm 16:16; 1 Cor 16:20; 2 Cor 13:12; 1 Pt 5:14; I Thess 5:26; Acts 20:37.

41. 1 Thess 3:6-7; 2 Jn 12; Phil 1:8; 2 Tim 1:4.

42. 2 Cor 2:4; 2 Tim 1:4; Acts 20:37. Cf. Jn 11:35-36.

43. Rm 1:7; 7:1, 4; 12:1; 16:8; 1 Cor 4:14; 4:17; 2 Cor 7:3; Eph 5:1; Phil 2:12; 4:1; 1 Thess 1:4; 2:8, 20; 2 Thess 2:13; 1 Tim 1:2; 2 Tim 1:2; Tit 1:4; Jam 1:19; 1 Pet 2:11; 4:12; 2 Pet 3:1, 14; 1 Jn 2:1, 7, 12, 14, 18, 28; 32; 4:1, 4, 7; 5:21; 3 Jn 1, 2, 5, 11; Jude 3, 17, 20.

44. 2 Cor 2:7-8.

45. Gal 6:1.

46. 2 Tim 2:24-25.

47. Lk 15:20.

48. A careful study of the gospels and epistles will reward the student with considerably more examples like those we have just mentioned.

49. Jn 17:21, 23.

50. See *L'Osservatore Romano,* Feb. 12, 1958, p. 1. We have discussed this idea in "The Superior's Precept and God's Will," *Review for Religious,* 1961, 20:439.

51. Gal 5:22-23.

52. CC #46.

53. Jn 13:34-35.

54. Heb 11:13.

55. CL #2.

56. Ps 63:1.

57. Pss 62:1; 73:25.

58. Ps 73:28.

59. Lk 9:3.

60. 2 Cor 6:10.

61. 1 Tim 6:7-8.

62. CC #8; DMAC #5.

63. CC #8; CCMW #1; DPOB #13.

64. DPOB #15; DMLP #17.

65. DMLP #17.

66. DRL #13.

67. CC #42; CCMW #36-37, 69, 72, 88.

68. Heb 11:13.
69. CL #2.
70. Col 3:1-2.
71. 2 Cor 4:17-18.
72. Jn 17:14-16.
73. Heb 11:13.
74. 1 Cor 7:29-32.
75. Isa 62:5.
76. 2 Cor 11:2.
77. Eph 5:21-33.
78. Gal 4:19; 1 Cor 4:14-15; 2 Cor 6:13; 2 Thess 2:7; Philemon 10; 1 Pet 5:13; 1 Jn *passim.*
79. Isa 62:4-5.
80. Ps 27:4.
81. Ps 62:1.
82. Ps 35:8.
83. Zeph 3:14, 17.
84. 2 Cor 11:2.
85. Eph 5:22-25, 28-30.
86. 1 Cor 7:32-35.
87. DMAC #18.
88. 1 Cor 6:17.
89. 1 Cor 7:35; DPOB #33.
90. St. Ambrose, "De virginibus," Bk 1, C 8; P. L. 16:203.
91. Ps 73:25, 28.
92. DPOB #33.
93. Jn 3:5-6.
94. 2 Cor 5:17; Eph 4:23-24.
95. Tit 3:4-7.
96. 1 Pet 1:23.
97. Jn 10:10.
98. 1 Cor 4:15.
99. 1 Jn 2:1, 7, 12, 14, 28; 3:2, 7, 18.
100. Gal 4:19.
101. For a more complete treatment of the sister's motherhood see our article, "Virginal Motherhood," *Review for Religious,* Sept., 1965, 24: 744-759.
102. 1 Cor 2:9.
103. 1 Cor 15:41-44. Cf. Phil 3:20-21; Mt 17:2.
104. 1 Cor 7:28.
105. 1 Cor 7:34.
106. 1 Cor 7:35.

107. Cf. Lk 12:48.
108. Phil 4:7.
109. Lk 18:29-30.
110. DRL #5.
111. DMAC #18.
112. CC #43.
113. DPOB #34.
114. CC #44; DRL #14.
115. CC #44, 42.
116. CC #46; DRL #1.
117. CC #44, 46; DRL #1, 12; DMAC #18.

NOTES FOR CHAPTER TWO

1. CL #2.
2. Lk 10:16.
3. Jn 14:26.
4. CC #12.
5. *Ibid.*
6. Karl Rahner, *Dynamic Element in the Church*, pp. 44-53.
7. We may incidentally note in this clause how the council regards the counsels as essential to religious life, a position incompatible with some current proposals.
8. CC #44.
9. *Ibid.*, #43.
10. DPOB #33.
11. DRL #2.
12. CC #46.
13. 1 Cor 7:34-35.
14. CL #2.
15. CC #44.
16. DRL #14.
17. DRL #8.
18. DRL #1; DPOB #33.
19. DRL #5.
20. CC #44.
21. DMAC #18.
22. DRL #6.
23. Jn 20:21.
24. DMAC #2.

25. DRF #2.
26. Ez 36:26-27.
27. 2 Cor 3:2-3.
28. Rm 8:2.
29. Jn 14:26.
30. Phil 2:13.
31. Jam 1:17.
32. 2 Cor 3:17.
33. Gal 5:18.
34. 1 Cor 13:4-7.
35. Gal 5:16, 22-23.
36. Jn 8:32-36 and Jn *passim*.
37. Gal 2:2, 6.
38. 2 Cor 6:10.
39. 1 Tim 6:7-8.
40. 1 Cor 2:2.
41. 2 Cor 7:4; Phil 2:17; 1 Thess 1:6; cf. 2 Cor 11:23-28.
42. Lk 14:33.
43. 2 Cor 3:17.
44. 1 Cor 7:32.
45. Ps 37:31.
46. Gal 5:16.
47. 2 Cor 3:2-3.
48. Jn 14:26.
49. Gal 5:22.
50. Ps 119:47, 97.
51. 1 Tim 1:9.
52. Ps 119:165.
53. Ps 119:45.
54. CC #43.
55. DRL #14.
56. Jn 8:32.
57. Rm 13:1-2.
58. 1 Pet 2:13; cf. Tit 3:1.
59. 2 Cor 5:14.
60. DMLP #22.
61. *Ibid.,* #15.
62. Lk refers to the elders as caring for "all the flock of which the Holy Spirit has made you the overseers, to feed the Church of God." Acts 20:28.
63. DRL #5.
64. 1 Pet 4:8.
65. Ps 119:10; Deut 6:5; Lk 10:27; Mt 5:48.

66. *Orthodoxy,* c. 4.

67. We have already pointed out that religious authority does not originate from the consent of the governed but from the universal jurisdiction possessed by the hierarchy. It is therefore ecclesial on this score also.

68. Rm 8:29; 1 Cor 1:30; 2 Cor 4:10; Gal 2:20; 3:27, 29; 4:13, 15; Phil 1:21. See also Rm 6:8; 8:1, 10; 13:14; 2 Cor 2:14, 15; Gal 1:22; Eph 3:17; Col 1:27; 3:4.

69. Lk 10:16.

70. 1 Thess 5:19-21.

71. Phil 2:7-8.

72. Ps 46:4-5.

73. Ps 48:1-2.

74. Ps 5:11.

75. Ps 4:3.

76. Ps 13:5.

77. Ps 21:6.

78. Ps 34:5, 8.

79. Ps 50:2.

80. Ps 16:11.

81. Ps 17:15.

82. Ps 36:8.

83. Ps 27:4.

84. Pss 40:16; 70:4.

85. Ps 84:2.

86. Pss 32:11; 64:10; 68:3; 97:11; 112:1; 128:1; 132:16.

87. Ps 1:2.

88. Pss 46:8; 66:5-7.

89. Ps 19:8, 10; 119:72, 92, 103.

90. Pss 107:1; 136 *in toto.*

91. Wis 13:3-5.

92. Ps 90:14.

93. Ps 95:1.

94. Ps 98:4.

95. Ps 105:2.

96. Ps 118:24.

97. Jn 15:11; 2 Jn 12.

98. 2 Cor 7:4; Phil 4:4.

99. 1 Pet 2:3-5.

100. 1 Cor 7:29-35.

101. One who denies this denies clear Catholic teaching. Documents of the magisterium could not be clearer.

102. Mt 19:29.

103. Ps 48:1-2.
104. Ps 84:2.
105. Ps 73:25-26, 28.
106. Lk 1:47.
107. 1 Cor 7:34-35.
108. CC #65.
109. Ps 73:25-26, 28.
110. 1 Pet 3:3-5.

NOTES FOR CHAPTER THREE

1. CL #2.
2. Mt 13:52.
3. CDR #8. Italics added.
4. Jn 14:26.
5. CDR #8.
6. 1 Cor 7:34, 35.
7. Ps 34:8; 1 Pet 2:2-5.
8. DPT #9. The Council is quoting St. Augustine, *In Joannem* 32:8; P. L. 35:1646.
9. Lk 10:16.
10. 1 Cor 3:16-17.
11. CC #8, 9, 13; DMAC #18, 22.
12. 1 Cor 13:1-3.
13. Ez 16:13-14.
14. Phil 2:2.
15. Phil 2:3.
16. 1 Cor 1:10.
17. Jn 17:21, 23.
18. Acts 4:32.
19. Phil 2:3.
20. Num 14:1-11. See also Ex 16:2, 8; Num 17:6-10.
21. Lk 10:16.
22. Rm 13:1-2.
23. Lk 8:4-15.
24. Mt 10:14-15.
25. Jn 3:19.
26. Cf., for example, 1 Cor 2:14; 2 Tim 4:3-4.
27. *Dynamic Element in the Church*, p. 47.
28. Mt 7:3-5.

29. 1 Mt 18:15.
30. Phil 2:1-2.
31. Acts 4:32.
32. DPT #9.
33. Lk 10:16.
34. 1 Cor 10:17.
35. Jn 6:56.
36. 1 Cor 3:16.
37. CL #2.
38. Matins, Jan. 21.
39. 1 Cor 7:32-35.
40. Jn 6:56.
41. Lk 22:19.
42. Gal 2:20.
43. 1 Cor 6:13, 17. "In the new covenant, through the giving ot His body in the Eucharist, Christ gives His total self-gift. In the covenant bond some members of the Church must give a like response by the gift of themselves through their bodies to Christ (whole Christ) in order that the covenant be fulfilled and that there be a focal point which reveals the meaning of a union which bears life. Thus, religious women become the Church in an intimate manner when they express in their religious profession, 'This is my body given for you.' In order to live at the heart of the Church and bear life to the Church by leading the Church to be woman, the religious woman must know and be herself as woman in the actions of virgin, bride, spouse and mother. As the Sister thus enters ever more deeply into the Paschal Mystery climaxed in the celebration of the Eucharistic sacrifice she is transformed into Christ, speaks Him ever more significantly to the world, and thereby, nourishes the life and growth of mankind into Christ."

Sister Mary Ann Follmar, F.S.P.A., unpublished communication to the present writer.
44. 1 Cor 11:26.
45. Lk 18:29-30.
46. Jn 13:34.
47. 1 Cor 1:10.
48. Phil 2:2.
49. Acts 4:32.
50. 1 Thess 4:9.
51. DMLP #18.
52. DMLP #5.
53. Col 3:3.
54. Ps 73:25-26, 28.
55. Ps 73:25.

56. Lk 14:33.
57. Eph 5:9.
58. Mt 5:48.
59. Lk 10:27.
60. CC #65.
61. DRL #5.
62. CDR #25.
63. CDR #7.
64. Ps 19:7-8.
65. Gal 4:19; 1 Cor 4:15.
66. Isa 55:10-11.
67. CL #2.
68. DPOB #33; CL #2; DRL #2.
69. CL #10.
70. CL #12; Mt 6:6; 1 Thess 5:17.
71. Phil 4:4-7.
72. DMAC #5.
73. Lk 22:19.
74. 1 Cor 7:34.
75. Eph 4:23.
76. *Ibid.*, v. 24.
77. Mt 16:25.
78. Jn 12:24.
79. Rm 6:5-6.
80. Mt. 6:31-33.
81. Lk 8:14.
82. Lk 14:33.
83. CC #31.
84. Cf. Karl Rahner, *Mission and Grace,* vol. 2, c. 8.
85. Ps 34:10.
86. Ps 62:5.
87. 1 Cor 1:23; 2:14.
88. Lk 24:25.
89. Phil 2:5-8.
90. Col 3:2-3.
91. The author gratefully acknowledges his debt for much of the thought and textual work of this paragraph to Sister M. Helen, O.S.C., Poor Clare of the Minneapolis community.
92. Gen 17:4, 7-8.
93. Gen 45:5, 7.
94. Ex 3:10.
95. Jd 6:12, 14.
96. Isa 6:9.

97. Jer 1:5, 7, 10.
98. Lk 1:16, 17.
99. Lk 2:30-31.
100. Mt 28:19-20.
101. DRL #5.
102. E.g., Lk 18:29-30.
103. See P. T. Camelot, "Virginity," *New Catholic Encyclopedia*, 14: 701.
104. DPT #10.
105. DRL #12.

NOTES FOR EPILOGUE

1. Lk 16:14-15.
2. 1 Cor 2:14.
3. We take it as obvious, of course, that specific practices in the religious life may not contradict sound psychology.
4. Hebr 13:8.

INDEX

VOCATIONAL PERSPECTIVES SERIES

1,
PERSONALISM AND VOCATION
Germain Lesage, O.F.M.

Father Lesage, of the University Seminary, Ottawa, Canada, analyzes the present vocation crisis and outlines what adaptations are necessary in religious life to fulfill the hopes and psychological needs of today's youth.

"An approach to the meaning and development of a vocation, and a frank look at the reasons why religious congregations are having a 'vocation crisis.'" Clear, specific and timely.

In its second printing.

$4.95

2.
NUNS, COMMUNITY PRAYER AND CHANGE
Sister Rosemarie Hudon, S.O.S.

It examines the prayer life of the nun in the context of the communal, spiritual and existential needs of the modern sister. After a splendid theological exposition on the meaning of prayer, the author surveys the forms, schedules and patterns which developed in convent life through the centuries down to today.

"Not only the communities of sisters to which the book is directly addressed, but also religious priests and brothers can surely profit much from this study. It is good theology and comes down to earth in its application." *Bernard Häring, C.Ss.R.*

In its fourth printing.

Ppr. $1.95

3.

THE NUN: SACRAMENT OF GOD'S SAVING PRESENCE
Gabriel Marie Cardinal Garrone

The purpose of this book is to reassess the place of the nun in the life of the Church. Aware of the contemporary criticisms of religious life, the author faces basic problems: shows why the nuns' role is unique, and probes the "means" whereby the nuns sanctify their lives —and become "signs of God" in a world which has lost the sense of his presence.

"An excellent series of meditations . . . on every important issue of the life of a religious in this modern world." *Sr. M. Bernetta, O.P.*

In its third printing.

Ppr. $1.95

4.

RESTRUCTURING RELIGIOUS LIFE
Patrick Berkery

This frank and open examination of the pressing problems in religious life indicates what changes (of structures and attitudes) are essential to the renewal of religious life.

"This book has the answers for those religious who still cannot grasp the idea of renewal and adaption." *Sr. Mary Rosalia, Greensburg Central Catholic High School, Greensburg, Pa.*

A selection of the Sister's Book League. In its second printing.

$3.95

5.

THE CHALLENGE OF "RADICAL" RENEWAL
Nicholas A. Predovich, S.J.

This is a radical book in the sense that it frankly and honestly faces the "root questions" which are now being faced, and must be faced, by all religious. The experienced author, eschewing a simplistic canonical approach to religious life, gets back to the scriptures as a starting point because old "canonized" answers seem evasive of the new questions: Is the traditional religious life totally obsolete today? Have the vows a meaning? How can we approach the "crisis of community" and related questions of obedience, authority, celibacy?

"The author has done the People of God a great service in his compact, imaginative, holistic, and sane re-evaulation of religious life during a time of renewal." *Peter J. Fleming, S.J., Alma College.*

$4.95

6.

POVERTY: SIGN OF OUR TIMES
Aloysius Schwartz

The author of THE STARVED AND THE SILENT makes an impassioned plea on behalf of the poor of the world and calls upon all to a renewal of the spirit and practice of the virtue of poverty as He preached it. A 16 page portfolio of photos is included.

$4.95

CHALLENGES OF LIFE
Ignace Lepp

This provactive and thoughtful study of man as he is today is based on the data of scientific experience.

The great themes which occur again and again in modern art and literature are illumnatingly presented. Adventure and risk, freedom and responsibility, the meaning of vocation, the call to growth, the need to keep responsive and openminded toward life, all these are discussed vigorously and clearly.

The author boldly faces up to the basic question of the very possibility of making a free choice, of being committed. Is man merely conditioned and determined? Can he raise above his situation whilst yet remaining in it? Is all this what can be said about sin, about fear, unrest, anxiety?

"This is a book that offers an intense insightful vision of life as an unending series of challenges by which man must grope his way toward God. It manages to communicate hope and enthusiasm for living, as well as the spiritual stimulation of listening to a truly wise, sensitive and optimistic human being . . . a rare piece of writing that has our unreserved recommendation." *The Register*

Book Club of the Month Selection—Sister's Book League, Thomas More Assoc.

$4.95